D1561435

RENEWAL
FOR THE
WOUNDED
WARRIOR

A Burnout Survival Guide for Believers

R. LOREN SANDFORD

Chosen

a division of Baker Publishing Group
Grand Rapids, Michigan

Published by Chosen Books
A division of Baker Publishing Group
P.O. Box 6287, Grand Rapids, MI 49516-6287
www.chosenbooks.com

Printed in the United States of America

Library of Congress Cataloging-in-Publication Data
Sandford, R. Loren.
    Renewal for the wounded warrior : a burnout survival guide for believers /
R. Loren Sandford.
        p.   cm.
    ISBN 978-0-8007-9480-4 (pbk.)
    1. Burn out (Psychology)—Religious aspects—Christianity. I. Title.
BV4509.5.S264 2010
248.8'6—dc22   2009034827

Unless otherwise noted Scripture quotations are from the New American Standard
Bible®, copyright © 1960, 1962, 1963, 1968, 1971, 1972, 1973, 1975, 1977, 1995 by The
Lockman Foundation. Used by permission.

10   11   12   13   14   15   16   7   6   5   4   3   2   1

In keeping with biblical principles of
creation stewardship, Baker Publishing Group advocates the responsible
use of our natural resources. As a
member of the Green Press Initiative,
our company uses recycled paper
when possible. The text paper of
this book is comprised of 30% post-
consumer waste.

"Contained within these pages is wisdom for your life's journey and lessons in the fear of the Lord—some of the best medicine anyone can receive. So take a spoonful of the Father's love and then chew and swallow the meat in this book, some gut-level truths that might just save your life."

"My first encounter with Loren Sandford came during a personal crisis in my life. I was experiencing burnout from ministry and had no one at that time with whom I felt safe sharing my feelings. Someone handed me a copy of Loren's book on burnout in ministry. This book helped me find the peace I was looking for while dealing with the emotional struggle I faced in co-pioneering an international ministry with my husband, Jack, a totally performance-driven burnout minister himself. Loren's transparency and willingness to open up his personal struggles with this issue gave me the courage I needed to seek healing and not become another casualty of ministry. I recommend this book, and feel that if ever there was a required reading list for ministers, this book should be on the list."

"Loren has been there; he knows that people in burnout have little energy to wade through complex prose or heed smug advice. Although this book is incredibly rich and deep, better yet it is an easy read and is user friendly."

This book is dedicated to my faithful and loving wife who stood by me without complaint through all the long years, patiently waiting for the changes God had promised in me. Her relentlessly positive nature and unwavering devotion to the Lord comprise a major portion of what has made this book possible.

CONTENTS

FOREWORD

Sometimes before you can get the right answer, you have to ask the right question. But often in today's instant success, fast food, pseudo-Christian, churchianity society, we are afraid even to admit we have a problem, let alone ask the right question. Sometimes we live in the longest river of the world: Denile.

Ever get the cart ahead of the horse? Put doing ministry ahead of ministering to the Lord? Come to the realization that you are serving the promotion of your own ministry instead of having an honest-to-God real relationship with your Maker and Creator?

I won't take a poll on that one, for if the truth be known, we have all walked down that path in one season or another. Some of us have not watched the gauges on the car and the oil light has been glaring at us for some time—glaring bright red until our vehicle comes to a full stop. Then it's *push* time. Yep, push the vehicle to make it seem as if we are still going somewhere.

Each of us needs to learn to take an honest assessment of our lives, our fruit, our expenditure. Jesus called it counting the cost before building the tower. I call it living in reality.

Do you think I know what I am talking about? Yes. Like you, I am still on a learning curve and need the help of others to point me in the right direction.

But help is on the way. God wants us to live a whole life—to be healed and to be holy. Many tools are coming together in our day in an integrated healing approach to life and ministry. One of these new tools is the book you hold in your hand.

Writing in a transparent style, R. Loren Sandford brings you lessons he has learned as the son of forerunners John Loren and Paula Sandford. Loren adds insights from his own experience, his own mistakes and his own revelation on this greatly overlooked subject.

So let's turn some lights on. Let's learn to yield the right of way to the wisdom of God's ways. Let's discover when to rebuke the enemy, when to stand firm—and yes, when to rest.

At this time in my life, the Holy Spirit has spoken to me that my highest weapon is *rest*. Now let's all rest. We will attempt to twist God's arm to find the newest recipe to rest. Right?

 No, it does not work that way. True rest is a Person. Resting in the everlasting arms of my Beloved—that is my cure and my key. What is yours?- ﹎. Job - 30 + 31 - Both of them.

Contained within these pages is wisdom for your life's journey and lessons in the fear of the Lord—some of the best medicine anyone can receive. So take a spoonful of the Father's love and then chew and swallow the meat in this book: some gut-level truths that might just save your life.

Warning: The contents of this book are healthy for the soul and will bring healing to the whole body. In fact, a new creation is about to occur!

In the trenches with you,

—James W. Goll
Encounters Network / Compassion Acts / Prayer Storm
author of *The Seer*, *The Coming Prophetic Revolution*,
The Lost Art of Practicing His Presence and many others

INTRODUCTION

For the last several decades burnout has been a much discussed and little understood condition both in the Christian world and outside of it. Help has focused largely on effecting remedial behavioral and lifestyle changes when pressures have spun out of control, but too little emphasis has been placed on the incapacity of the burnout victim to make those changes. Much of what has been written has therefore been of little real help to those whose experience has left them both deeply wounded and marginally functional.

Up to a point, behavioral changes can help restore strength and enable a wounded one to continue in labor, life and ministry. For many of us, however, the truth is that behavioral changes do not help—even when we have the strength to make them—and that burnout serves only to soften us up for the deeper things God really has in store. Burnout can actually serve a helpful function in breaking through denial systems and structures of performance built over a lifetime to protect roots of wounding, fears and strongholds acquired so early in life that we rarely consciously recognize their presence. In my personal experience I recovered from burnout and enjoyed two good years of restored vitality only to discover that the real work had yet to begin by means of a wilderness experience neither I nor anyone around me understood.

Therefore, while the first part of this book addresses issues related to burnout, the second part plumbs the depths of the dark night of the soul. As opposed to burnout brought on by life and its circumstances, the dark night of the soul is a time of suffering and loss sent by the hand of God to deal with the deep reaches of our nature and character, even the parts we had forgotten or that we thought had been well sanctified. The dark night of the soul looks and feels different from burnout and demands a different set of responses. The burnout years taught me what some of those responses needed to be, and that time of burnout built them into my character. I later learned that in burnout I had experienced nothing more than a rehearsal for events that would later test those elements of character to their limit.

This book is deeply confessional in nature. Much self-disclosure and personal experience went into it. A church member once commented that my willingness to share my experience of brokenness demonstrates my humility, but I have never considered myself a humble man. Quite the contrary! I simply believe that my life experience should help others understand their own passages. Some have deemed me courageous for baring so much of my soul and my life. What courage? What have I to hide? What could I lose that has not already been lost? I pose these questions rhetorically, not in sarcasm or complaint, but from a place of rest brought about by the experience of the dark night of the soul.

Ultimately, does anything but Jesus really matter? If that sounds a bit trite, understand that things that once seemed overly simplistic to me have taken on a whole new depth of meaning. On top of that, maintaining an acceptable public persona in false honor consumes a great deal of energy. I no longer have that to spend—and it really is as simple as the Person of Jesus.

What I have written concerning the purposes of God in the wilderness—or the dark night of the soul—may be threatening to some who make no room in their theology for the concept of redemptive suffering. I did not write this book to start a debate, nor will I engage in one. Suffice it to say that those who have lived what I describe in these pages will understand my message and, I hope, take heart for the outcome of their own wilderness sojourns.

I have written as briefly as possible and sought an easy reading style, knowing that those worn down by deep suffering often have neither the patience nor the energy for extended reading or lengthy scholarly presentations. I intended this book to be both accessible and understood by those who suffer most deeply. I pray it provides the encouragement I hoped for because precious little encouragement is available anywhere in the Christian world. The Body of Christ seldom deals well with those who suffer for extended periods of time. Few counselors, much less the Body of Christ at large, truly understand the problem unless they have lived it. As the old saying goes, "It takes one to know one." But God does have answers. Scripture speaks to these issues in ways both healing and true to reality.

More than the emotional impact, both burnout and the dark night of the soul take a frightening toll on physical health and well-being. Often sufferers have visited the family doctor for any number of associated physical symptoms and been given a clean bill of health. They come away discouraged and confused because the aches, pains and ills they experience are very real and truly do hinder their ability to function. Unfortunately, medical science has no means of measuring these things until sufferers are threatened by catastrophic breakdown.

The "faith," "success in life" and "word of faith" teachings so prevalent in our Christian subculture constitute cruel medicine for the burnout victim who already feels as if he or she has failed. To the one in the dark night of the soul these teachings stand so beyond relevance as to seem laughable, naive or even cruel. Those for whom I have written have often reached such a point of emotional and physical weakness as to be incapable of meeting the demands these performance-oriented teachings make of them. They simply cannot "believe" any longer or "confess" as they ought.

This leads to an overwhelming sense of failure and guilt. Although offered in innocence and with a genuine desire to help, these "faith" teachings often have a way of visiting crippling condemnation on those who really need an ample dose of mercy and grace. The deeply wounded can no longer find their answers in method. If they need a theology preached to them, it must be a compassionate one that makes sense of redemptive suffering, not a performance-oriented system of religious thought laced with condemnation for failure. They must be lifted and carried in a tender way that gives much and asks little.

Their faith has been shaken to the core and often shattered. Exhausted spiritually, emotionally and physically, they can no longer lift themselves out of the depths by any personal effort at right thinking or acting. Some have despaired even of the knowledge that God truly loves them. Filled with fear that their fatigue, anxiety, failure and pain will be exposed and condemned, they therefore keep to themselves in a dangerous form of withdrawal that invites disaster on a number of fronts.

Frequently, inner pressures of hurt and despair combine with the continuing demands of day-to-day life, labor or ministry to produce a devastating breakdown. Rather than respond with restorative compassion, the Body of Christ too often beats the wounded one to death with religious platitudes and backstabbing suspicions. Years ago a friend of mine said that the Body of Christ is the only army in the world that shoots its wounded. How true!

To those teetering on the brink, bleeding and fearful—clergy, lay leaders and believers struggling with life's tests—I say that you are not alone, that you are not hopeless and that God has a merciful plan to move you through the wilderness and into your promised land. *God has not abandoned you. You have not lost your anointing or His presence.* You may not be able to sense the direction or the outcome, but God is moving you toward glory.

I realize that both women and men suffer in the ways I describe in this book, and for the same reasons. I do, however, find inclusive language to be insufferably tedious and painfully artificial in certain contexts. Please realize, therefore, that most of my uses of the masculine include the feminine.

Finally, I have found the material in this book to be helpful both to clergy and lay leaders and to as many as are deeply affected by stress or despair, no matter what walk of life they occupy. Anyone who suffers the effects of long-term stress from any cause will find something useful here. I speak from the perspective of a ministry professional, but the basic causes and symptoms of burnout and of the wilderness experience remain the same at any level of calling and for any walk of life.

PART I

BURNOUT

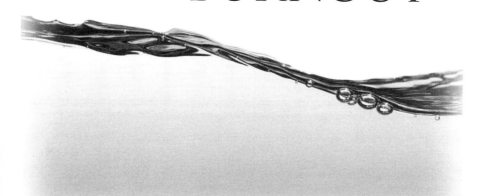

I hurl my questions high and sing into forever
I wait for answers why
Sometimes it seems like never
Somewhere light glows
Somewhere love flows
And there's a place where the air is clear
A place of wind in the angel's hair
It's gonna be all right
Somewhere tears dry
Somewhere dreams fly

I hear the sound of a rushing wind
To fan the flames on our heads again
It's gonna be all right
I hurl my questions high and sing into forever
I wait for answers why
Sometimes it seems like never
And then . . .

Somewhere light glows
Somewhere love flows
And there's a place where the air is clear
A place of wind in the angel's hair
It's gonna be all right

1

THREE KINDS OF DAMAGE

Especially among professionals of various kinds, *burnout* has become a term commonly heard. Its use reflects a heightened awareness—for some perhaps desperation—concerning a widespread problem among those who expend themselves in the service of others or who occupy positions of responsibility in life or in the working world. The problem extends beyond those in leadership. Whether or not you occupy a position of responsibility, life can serve up crises in such rapid succession as to allow insufficient time to recover from one crisis or loss before being forced to absorb the impact of the next one.

Three kinds of damage can result, only one of which could be called burnout. Depression and wounding complete the list. Each of these feeds into and affects the others so that any effective approach to healing must account for all three.

A Definition of Burnout

For the present purpose I will differentiate burnout from depression and wounding by saying that burnout happens only to those who can be characterized as givers at some level. Burnout develops when the physical and emotional resources that enable the giver to keep giving have been depleted. This leads to despair, depression, irrational anger and a host of physical problems.

In the intensity of their giving, "burnouts" care too little about—or have too little consciousness of—their personal needs to do what must be done to replenish their spiritual, emotional and physical resources. The cause of this failure can often be traced to performance orientation, or it can be as simple as living through one or more seasons of high demand experienced by any of us who minister or lead in the church, in the family or in the world. A period of rest can often cure simple burnout, but the same is seldom true of depression and wounding.

A Definition of Depression

Depression is an emotional manifestation of the depletion of one's physical and emotional resources for dealing with stress. It can happen to anyone, giver or not, who faces extended unrelenting stress without the time, the ability or, in some cases, the willingness to process it in a healthy way. In its most extreme form, depression can become so debilitating as to render the sufferer unable to function. Paralyzed, he or she cannot in any way summon the energy to cope with life or respond to its demands. For such people, hopelessness has become their total environment.

Performance orientation, together with the physical and emotional stress it creates, triggers depression more than almost any other cause. Unable to conceive of themselves as loved or accepted apart from meeting certain standards and expectations, performance-oriented people suffer from a grace deficit. Their hope of love, as well as their ability to accept themselves, centers around efforts to successfully meet

20

certain behavior or productivity criteria—imposed by others or internal to the individual.

Unfortunately, this fear motivation for living and achieving exacts a terrible physical and emotional toll. The result can be deep depression until the victim learns that self-acceptance, God's love and love from others come through the gift of grace that can only be received and not earned.

A Definition of Wounding

Wounding is an emotional condition, a form of stress, caused by the hurtful acts of others. Just as the physical body draws upon finite and exhaustible resources to meet the daily demands of life, so our emotions consume limited stores of human strength as we meet and deal with the lumps life serves up for the heart. Once these resources have been depleted, devastation and desperation result. As part of living in this world, any person can and will suffer occasional emotional wounding. This can take the form of a death in the family, serious illness, job loss and a host of other stresses that cause us to reach deep into our inner stores of strength. For givers by nature or by profession, however, the damage can be especially severe when those they serve become the cause of their pain and when that pain has been inflicted consistently over time.

For those involved in giving professions, it simply will not do to speak of professional detachment as a remedy or protection. To minister true healing, we must love. To love, we must risk ourselves at some level. This principle holds true both for those who engage in ministry and for those who take responsibility for people in other care settings. In any healing encounter there must be a meeting of persons. Any true meeting of persons necessarily involves a level of vulnerability for both parties. That being understood, when one for whom you have poured forth your life turns on you with fangs bared, the pain can be overwhelming while the energy required to process it can be enormous.

Normally, life serves up its hurts, losses, betrayals and abandonments at a pace that allows time for recovery and restoration between episodes. Occasionally, however, these wounds come in such rapid succession or touch us too deeply to allow for effective recovery between onslaughts. Wreckage results in the form of physical illness, depression, withdrawal or isolation, paranoia and fear of emotional betrayal, wounding or other forms of damage.

Conclusion

Obviously, significant areas of overlap and interrelationship exist between burnout, depression and wounding, in both cause and effect. In this chapter I have differentiated between them only to emphasize that the condition I am ultimately addressing is a great deal more serious and complex than the kind of thing many of us have become accustomed to reading about in books and professional journals on burnout. The pain suffered by so many goes much deeper than can be accounted for by the mere depletion of energies. For this reason appropriate remedies most often involve more than just rearranging schedules and prioritizing activities. Having made this point concerning the differences between burnout, depression and wounding, I will henceforth use the terms interchangeably in most contexts.

For the sake of discussion I have divided the process of falling into burnout into three progressive stages. In turn, I will examine each of these stages of burnout in three sections: the first describing the physical symptoms evident at that stage, the second addressing the emotional condition of the sufferer and the third suggesting what sort of ministry can be appropriately offered by those who wish to help.

2

STAGE ONE
BURNOUT—ONSET

Physical Symptoms

Have you wondered where your strength has gone? Do you feel it beginning to slip away? Here are some bodily symptoms, warning signs of trouble to come.

Chronic Fatigue and Costly Errors

In the early stages of burnout, the sufferer may experience chronic fatigue and require noticeably longer periods of recovery following severe exertions of time and energy. This especially holds true for those engaged in ministry to others when crises such as funerals, interpersonal conflicts and commitments demanding extra investments of time and energy (like conferences and summer camps) begin to pile up. For those in lay positions or who face life in general when demands and stresses mount, the same principle holds true. Where recovery once came about quickly—perhaps a day or two of sleeping in—a week or two passes before feeling right again.

Just getting up in the morning becomes more and more difficult for the early burnout victim. Refreshment eludes him or her so that whole days often pass in a constant battle against sleepiness. The victim must push to keep moving.

Despite daytime fatigue, falling asleep at night becomes increasingly difficult. Even when sleep comes quickly, the night is seldom restful. The mind refuses to let go of things and races on and on, resisting every effort to control it. At first the victim may dismiss this as part of being gifted: "I do my most creative thinking in bed before I go to sleep." This may be true, but in reality it clearly indicates a degree of performance orientation that renders the victim unable to let go of things and find peace. In the later stages of burnout, creativity will die out, buried under layers of stress and obsessive worry. At this early stage, dreams will become increasingly labored or troubled so that the sufferer wakes in the morning feeling as if he has been at work all night.

Tired people make more mistakes than healthy people. Thought processes slow down, or they accelerate to the point that actions and decisions are not carefully thought through. Stress and fatigue distort perceptions of reality resulting in responses to events that are often less well considered than they normally would be. Errors of judgment in ministry, business, various kinds of administration and personal relationships inevitably multiply. This most directly affects sensitive relationships like friends and family that we all so desperately need for maintaining health and balance in life. Vital support systems therefore suffer damage, which only serves to exacerbate the problem of stress overload. Physical fatigue leads to costly emotional and administrative error.

For instance, early in the history of the first church I planted in 1980 we encountered an enormous need that would require a great deal of money. I knew we did not have those resources, that we had no means of acquiring them and that it was a need we could postpone dealing with until those resources could be accessed. One brother with a history of household financial failure kept pestering me with a foolish and impractical proposal after I had called an end to the discussion. He persisted until I blurted, "This from a man who has filed bankruptcy!" just to put him off and hoping to joke or tease him into dropping the subject. Wrong! Instantly I flushed hot with shame. Under normal circumstances I would never have allowed myself to say anything so stupid and ill considered, much less allow a clearly hurtful word to come out of my mouth. Damage control took a long time. In my weariness I wounded someone I cared about.

Because the burnout victim, even in the early stages, sometimes fails to accurately hear things said to him through the fog of fatigue, he may occasionally respond inappropriately to those who present needs or ask questions. As I did, he may mean to tease a friend in a loving way, but it comes out sounding like a hurtful insult. Or the sufferer may forget to include important people in crucial planning and then must suffer their sense of rejection or anger over being left out.

All of this opens the door to the critical spirit that lurks about seeking opportunity to tear apart families, churches and workplaces. As tongues begin to wag, the burden of stress grows, becoming a heavier and heavier drag on the budding burnout victim. In my lifelong position of leadership I have learned that for every person I offend in some way an "army" of ten to twenty waits to be secondarily offended as they pass the story around. As a result, people begin to see the burnout victim through a filter of offense and prejudice that leads them to assign evil motives and to accuse the burnout victim of all manner of abuse and insensitivity.

Such talk creates a negative spiritual pressure on the ministry—or the workplace or the home—that tends to lock up anointing and hinder effectiveness. Not even Jesus could do many miracles in His hometown because of the offense the local people took at Him. The burnout sufferer knows firsthand the truth of what Jesus faced. More stress results.

Tension Reactions

Lockjaw! My personal "favorite" tension reaction. How my teeth survived the pressure of burnout remains a mystery. Other symptoms might include chronic muscle tension in the shoulders or other areas. Unconscious nervous tapping of the hands and feet may develop. Twitching muscles in the face or elsewhere may become habitual. To this day I have a problem with chronic headaches that began during my early burnout years—not an uncommon symptom.

Many of us find that tension lodges in the digestive system. Early symptoms of colitis may appear at this time as chronic pain in the lower abdomen. This can include recurring bouts with irregularities in bowel movements. Problems with acid indigestion and stomach ulcers may develop.

Emotional Condition

Many of us live and work in situations where anxiety is regarded as essential to performance. In fact, persistent anxiety may be a precursor to significant dysfunction. In the first stage of burnout the seeds of emotional breakdown that have been sown over time begin to germinate and show up in a variety of ways.

Vague Fear and Anxiety

More than anything else, the sufferer will notice an increasing awareness of, or struggle with, fear and anxiety, often not attributable to any known cause except perhaps the occasional anticipation of a situation in which performance will be required. At this stage, such anxiety can be temporarily eclipsed by the intensity of ministry anointing, by an adrenaline rush or by an accelerated pace of life that leaves no room for thinking. Because of the slight edge adrenaline gives, this kind of fear may even contribute to enhanced performance for a time, but I promise that this benefit will pass. It may take the form of fear of failure, fear of the unknown, fear of attack, or any other sort of fear, but the ability to deal with and subdue it has begun to erode.

In the early stages of wounding, nagging questions arise concerning one's faith and personal relationship with God that seem to have no satisfactory answers. The early burnout victim nervously ponders questions like, "Is the counseling I'm doing really effective? Are people really being changed? Will I ever receive or achieve the things I believe God has promised me? Will the problems I face ever be overcome? Is God really here for me?" In spite of this, he or she still hopes deeply and can encourage others with that hope even as the ability to live creatively with these questions begins to weaken.

Prayer Life

Prayer life probably remains intact at this stage. Daily devotions remain a source of refreshment and of conversation with God, but dry times occur more frequently and tend to last longer. Perhaps more significantly, fatigue, the pressure of daily life and the demands of people begin to cut into available prayer time and the sufferer feels powerless to stop it. This often develops during what seem to be wonderful periods of growth and anointing. In the glow of success or the excitement of forward motion, warning signs can be easily ignored.

Confidence Remains

In stage one burnout, confidence in personal ability, anointing and strength remain, if confidence was where he or she began. My wife repeatedly warned me concerning how much energy I was spending without giving myself adequate time to rest. Confident and trusting in my own strength, I protested, "I have a course to run, Beth, and I don't have God's permission to stop yet. The job isn't done!" We had started a new church and were laying foundations, building people up and experiencing all the intensity of investment that comes with assembling a new Body of Christ out of the spiritual wilderness.

On the one hand, I know I was right, and in the same situation I would say the same thing to her again. On the other hand, with the benefit of years of hard-won wisdom, the spirit of my reply would now be different, as would the spirit of my efforts. No matter how demanding the work might be, there would be a peace in it that I could scarcely imagine when I was younger. I was headed for a train wreck and could not see it coming.

In this early stage the anointing of the Lord does sustain you in spite of fatigue, but more and more often you run on adrenaline strength, sometimes not recognizing the difference between adrenaline rush and the anointing of God. Understanding the difference is a function of wisdom, and wisdom comes only through time and suffering.

In stage one, the individual entering burnout begins to shave healthy, self-renewing activities such as recreation and exercise from his schedule. He may even feel a bit noble about it, glorying in the delusionary sense that he is wearing himself out in the service of the Lord. And it is true! He really does love the Lord, but work and its related stresses leave little energy for fun and personal replenishment. The care of his physical "temple" suffers. And our reasons for engaging in such self-destructive patterns are never so pure as we want to believe.

Ministry Realities in Stage One

At this point, normal ministry remains possible. A stage one burnout victim can still engage in the kind of interaction with others that is so necessary to most healing. You can speak with him about root causes of his condition and he can respond, recognize his sin and pray wonderfully well in relation to it. He can shed tears and thank you for his deliverance. Afterward he may make some attempts to adjust his lifestyle, but those who minister to the burnout victim should expect these attempts to be short-lived in the long run. Most likely he already knows what must be done to avoid the inevitable, but he either cannot or will not do it.

As was the case with me, by this time self-destructive patterns have probably become too strong, too pervasive and too deeply cloaked in denial to be easily or quickly broken. More than likely, the victim of early-onset burnout will have to ride those patterns to the bottom before the delusions they represent will be fully exposed and their power defeated. He or she will have to burn out on being burned out.

At this point in my own life I knew I had a task to perform from which I could not turn aside and with which I felt I had too little real help. That much was true, but deep-seated fears of rejection and failure drove me, of which I was almost completely unaware. That combination of pressures and fears prevented me from slowing down long enough to deal with my own needs in a life-changing way. Real healing remained out of reach until the course had been run and the task finished. The finishing nearly killed me, and in the end I felt I failed anyway.

Prevention?

Conventional wisdom focuses on prevention of burnout. Having lived it, I question whether or not this is always the wisest approach or even the will of God. What if God actually allows burnout to occur as a tool for crucifying the flesh and subsequently resurrecting His servants into new life? Could it be that sometimes the only tool we "blockheads" leave Him to work with is the experience and aftermath of going down in flames?

Burnout burns away old patterns, ungodly attitudes and fleshly ways of approaching life and people. Even had I known how to stop my downward slide in its early stages, I probably would not have done it. Through it all I retained the mysterious sense that the hand of God was leading me down this path and that if I simply embraced the pain I would learn wisdom from it. I was right. Jesus is Lord. I did not know, however, how much pain I would ultimately be asked to embrace.

Not Yet the Dark Night

In the early stages of burnout I naively thought my experience was "the dark night of the soul." Wrong! I had not yet even begun. Especially if you possess a dynamic personality, you begin your ministry filled with boundless energy, talents and abilities. In those early stages you have neither the wisdom nor the experience to understand the difference between anointing and natural strength. No matter what you think or acknowledge theologically concerning the sin of man, you really have no idea how far short of the nature of Jesus your own character falls. It has not yet become important for you to be fully aware of this because the issue of prime importance at this stage is growth in knowledge and understanding. Holy awareness of limitations comes later.

You therefore confidently soldier on while everything you touch seems to turn to gold because of the anointing of God on your life and because of the wisdom He has taught you. But then He begins to strip it all away. Nothing works anymore. God seems far off and you begin to question everything you thought you knew. You can suffer burnout but remain successful. You can burn out and things may still work for you, at least for a while, but the dark night of the soul takes you beyond burnout and into a darker place. The dark night of the soul brings you to the cross where you cannot escape until you learn that you have nothing in yourself and that He has it all. The dark night burns away the flesh until you know that only the Spirit makes you live.

Until that point, you can do little more than hold your heart open to the searingly bright light of His presence and choose to endure the pain and brokenness His purity creates in your flesh. God, as you encounter Him in the dark night of the soul, does not look like the God you thought you knew. At first, none of this darkness seems like light, but light it is.

That which I at first regarded as the dark night of the soul was in truth nothing more than Act One, Scene One. It set the stage for what came later. Burnout weakened me, but it did not expose my deepest fears and flaws, nor did it fundamentally change me. That came much later, in a real dark night of the soul.

Embracing the Pain

As I stated earlier, I hold limited concern for preventing burnout. My reason? I find little value in preserving the flesh. Therefore, from start to finish, from burnout to dark night, this suffering must be accepted, embraced and seen through to its end. Though he may not be aware of it, the stage one burnout victim has been running hard in his natural strength and continues to do so. God has ordained a course to bring this to a holy end.

3

STAGE TWO BURNOUT—
BREAKDOWN BEGINS

Physical Symptoms

As a former bodybuilder, I know what happens when muscles have been overworked. Body parts need time to recover between stresses. When muscles have been overworked, they weaken, spasm and ache. The same is true of every organ in the body. Unrelenting stress causes body parts and internal organs to overwork without the benefit of restorative periods of rest. As with overworked muscles, this produces painful symptoms according to the functioning of each affected organ.

Adrenal Burnout

I am no physician. I know only what I have been told by those who care for my body professionally. Adrenal burnout occurs when the adrenal gland has been overproducing for such a long time that it can no longer function as it was designed to function. Whereas stress once created an adrenaline "rush" that could be used to enhance performance or heighten the enjoyment of an experience, it now often produces a sensation of sickness, like trying to start a car in cold weather on a nearly dead battery.

In fact, the sufferer has become stress-addicted. Subconsciously, she actually needs and creates stressful situations so that the fear, pressure and resulting adrenaline production overcome her fatigue. But adrenaline no longer gets her moving as it once did. The "rush" has vanished. Increasingly, situations that once produced an energizing effect now make her feel sick and angry.

For example, from time to time I used to find myself in unexpected possession of a free day for sermon preparation early in the week. Rather than take advantage of it to reduce my stress load, I almost subconsciously found ways to fill up that free time so that I would be pressured and stressed on Saturday. Why? Because I *needed* pressure and stress.

"I work better under pressure." Have you ever heard anyone make that claim? Those who make such assertions are good candidates for burnout. Given a light workload, I tended to produce mediocre work, but in an overload situation I worked like a madman at the peak of my form and excellence. I *needed* stress to function effectively. Without it, I struggled with the paralyzing effects of fatigue. One of the recovering alcoholics in my congregation once asked me, "Are you addicted to adrenaline flow?" Sadly, I had to answer yes.

At stage two in the process of degeneration, stress addiction begins to fail as a motivator and energizer. The burnout victim begins to accept fatigue as an unpleasant fact of life—a given. Many burnout victims then find it difficult to remember, or even to imagine, life without exhaustion.

Digestive Disturbances

Digestive disturbances become common at this stage, attacking whatever happens to be the weakest link in the system. This can result in a variety of physical breakdowns, including painful stomach ulcers and colon disorders. The colon registers stress more readily than almost any other organ. As a result, colitis may flair up and cause extreme pain. Diarrhea is common. Food allergies may develop. The digestive system reacts to stress by producing more acid and other chemicals than God designed the system to process. As a result it becomes overly sensitive even to minor irritants that it might easily have thrown off before stress took its toll.

Sleep Difficulties

❚ Not only does sleep become occasionally difficult, it becomes a labor. Mentally and emotionally we often process stress in the form of dreams. I recall dreaming night after night of being engaged in a battle in which I had no power over my enemy. In these dreams every movement felt like swimming through cold molasses, every stroke of my sword or thrust of my fist deprived of force. Or I might find myself in combat without my sword and swinging at my enemy with an imaginary one. I even made swooshing noises to make it seem more powerful.

After a night of such fruitless warfare, I awakened drained and sick. Sleeping became so difficult that I deliberately stayed up late, night after night, partly to reach such a point of fatigue that I would sleep quickly and soundly when I finally surrendered and went to bed.

General Physical Illness

In general, physical illness becomes more common in stage two. For instance, colds may be caught more frequently and linger much longer. Sore throats may develop several times each year and take ages to overcome. Aches and pains proliferate mysteriously. Headaches increase in frequency and intensity. Chronic stress weakens the immune system.

The sufferer may notice that his physical tension reactions to ministry or work situations have intensified. My sinuses used to swell shut while my eyes felt as though they wanted to cross whenever I faced an afternoon of back-to-back counseling appointments. Often I found myself nodding off to sleep in the middle of someone's tearful outpouring of woe and I would silently cry out to God to please make it stop. I learned to yawn without opening my mouth. I wondered if I had become physically allergic to ministry. I found that if I drank enough coffee before I began my counseling day, I could make it through, but this produced both negative side effects and diminishing returns.

Emotional Condition

At this stage I found myself hating books like *Power in Praise* by Merlin Carothers. Everyone I knew wanted me to read it, thinking it would be the remedy to the pit I felt beginning to swallow me up. Good book! I highly recommend it, but at this stage teachings like this only made me angry. No matter how I tried, I found myself incapable of doing what the book called for—at least not consistently. Emotional symptoms multiply at this stage, to the point that the sufferer often feels powerless to turn the tide.

Anxieties

Anxiety consumes more and more of the sufferer's thoughts, growing into a near constant and becoming harder to ignore. The sufferer may be overwhelmed by fear that the ministry, his business or other endeavors will fail, that too many things are going wrong in ways he feels powerless to correct. Life in general may seem to be careening out of control. When will the next blow fall? Who will deliver it? Betrayals and setbacks appear larger than life, and restoration of perspective requires a major exercise of mental discipline.

For example, as a burden bearer by nature, I feel the emotions of those around me almost as if they were my own, much like Counselor Troi, the empathic Betazoid on the television series *Star Trek: The Next Generation*. In my spirit I can sense how my church is doing at any given time, aware at an instinctive level when discord has flared up or when trouble of some other kind threatens, even when two thousand miles away on a speaking trip.

During this stage of burnout, no matter how badly I needed to, I could not shut down or balance these senses. Instinctively sensing when tongues had begun to wag in the church, I found myself gripped by fear in a way that distorted my perception of reality. Although I retained enough strength to govern how I outwardly responded to what I felt, I had lost the ability to control it internally and remain balanced. I knew in advance when personal attacks were developing and then suffered a double wounding by reason of fearful anticipation when they actually materialized. Cognitive distortions that make things seem bigger than they really are become a serious problem at this stage.

As a pastor I even feared that my anointing might expire. God never let me down or abandoned me, but I feared such loss just the same. Road trips for ministry engagements around the country became welcome respites from pressure and fear in the home ministry. At home it seemed I floundered in powerlessness, but in foreign places overwhelmingly positive responses buoyed my sinking sense of gifting. In the same way, leaders in secular settings may be tempted to retreat into any manner of legal and illegal refuges where some sense of relief from powerlessness can be obtained.

Erosion of Confidence

At last, therefore, the wounded one's basic sense of confidence and competence comes under assault. Whether in life, labor or ministry, he feels as if he works from an empty bucket that never gets refilled. Confidence gives way to desperation as again and again he goes to the well for strength and wisdom to meet the needs and demands of others and of life itself, only to find little or nothing there to draw upon.

As he loses perspective on the true significance of failures and setbacks, he finds himself unable to take encouragement from successes as he once did. In fact, he may become functionally blind to the goodness in his life, ministry or labor. Nothing anyone says has the power to penetrate that perception and to keep him on track.

Ministry, management of life, going to work every day becomes a struggle against unrelenting pain, interspersed with episodes of joy and sanity. Increasingly, requests for time and energy provoke angry responses internally that the burnout victim struggles to conceal—or not, depending on his character. Every church or business has its leeches who consume vast amounts of time and energy for little or no apparent return or purpose. The burnout victim may never have learned the fine art of prioritizing which individuals constitute a good investment and which ones simply consume for no good return. As a result, those healthy leaders and workers who would share the burden receive neither adequate nurture nor opportunity to grow. This leaves the burden resting heavily upon the weary shoulders of the burnout victim.

Withdrawal and Isolation

Episodes of withdrawal and isolation become more frequent, with heightened intensity and extended duration. Because the victim has so little energy left with which to manage demands of any kind, she withdraws even from family and friends. In this state, even offers of love may seem to be demands for a response of some kind so that, instead of feeling refreshed by the love of those close to her, she may actually feel drained by it.

In her work setting, people around her may exacerbate the problem by complaining that she does not seem as warm, engaging or attentive as she once did. For example, circumstances may prevent her from being present for a crisis or two. This leads those affected by the crisis to attack her in private conversation because they could not understand her absence and felt it unjustified.

She begins to wonder angrily if people would be satisfied only if she gashed herself and gave them her very lifeblood. What sacrifice would finally be enough? In a ministry situation, if she has always been a physically affectionate person, people may begin to feel that her hugs are not as real as they once were, if she still gives them at all. It may become apparent that she fails to listen as well as she once did. All this can provoke negative and critical talk in the people she leads. Obviously this adds to the burden of stress that has been slowly killing her.

Some burnout victims may begin to stay up late at night to find the time alone that they feel they so desperately need. Even today in my own case, having both an acute spiritual awareness and a burden-bearing nature, I can feel the people to whom I minister drawing on me spiritually and emotionally until about 10:00 P.M. when they begin to go to bed. At that hour I can actually sense them letting go of me, and by 11:00 P.M. I find myself blissfully alone in every way and longing to stay up later and later to enjoy it.

When in withdrawal mode, those late-night hours become *my* time. Obviously, however, morning never comes any later. Abbreviated hours of sleep ultimately make the problem worse. Others in this condition might go to bed early and get up early for the same reasons. The wounded one feels driven to find that time in solitude by whatever means can be made to work.

Rage at God, a Crisis of Faith

Episodes of rage at God can become common. The second stage burnout victim feels increasingly abandoned and betrayed by Him. In the burnout victim's eyes God has failed to be the protector He promised He would be. At an emotional level he feels God has failed to keep His promises and concludes that fulfillment will never come. He may often feel as though God is present for others through him, but seldom for him personally. God has let him down.

In 1980 I planted Cornerstone Christian Fellowship in Post Falls, Idaho, sandwiched between Spokane, Washington, on the west and Coeur d'Alene, Idaho, on the east. From the start, we felt that God had given us a number of prophecies for that church concerning growth and destiny in ministry. As time passed, many of those promises were delayed while many never came to pass at all. Beginning with our first service of worship, God allowed us a double dose of troublemakers who went right to work attacking me and distorting my every word and action. It seemed that when they could not find something legitimate to twist and blow out of proportion, they simply made something up and then convinced themselves that what they had made up was true. A long time passed before they left the church. While they remained in our midst, their influence kept us from realizing any of the promises God had given us.

Under the combined weight of these betrayals by people and God's delay in fulfilling promises, I experienced episodes of such deep wounding that I angrily began to accuse God of being a liar, betrayer and promise-breaker. Because I could no longer bear up under the pain of being repeatedly let down, I actually prayed that He would promise me nothing more ever again.

Needless to say, prayer life begins to suffer at this stage and becomes a roller coaster of ups and downs. Occasionally God comes through with such intimacy and blessing that you feel like a fool for all the anger you held, but increasingly the prayer closet becomes a place of pain and alienation where you remember that God has not kept His promises and has not protected you from strife and disaster. As a result, you pray less.

The wounded one in stage two can still hope—and does so in blessed episodes of light and freedom—but the ability to sustain it quickly fades. Periods of despair become both common and paralyzing.

Breakdown of Emotional Control

As emotional control breaks down, the sufferer finds himself subject to sudden impulses to weep over small things. My family has always joked about my disdain for fictional children's features like *Winnie the Pooh* or *101 Dalmatians*. When my children were little, the family teased me every time one of these came on the television and I found myself forced to watch it with them. At this stage of burnout, try as I might, I could not hide the tears. Giggling, the kids often caught me leaking over things like a bunch of spotted cartoon puppies coming home after a life-threatening odyssey! Greater emotional freedom remains one of the lasting legacies of my burnout years. In contrast to my former rigid emotional control, today my oldest daughter jokes about me, "Dad cries over everything!"

At this point in my downward slide, I might be found secretly tuning in to the Disney Channel late at night to sniffle over the sorrows of some ridiculous animated character, wondering what on earth could be the matter with me. In truth, I carried so many stored-up and unresolved hurts and tensions that it did not require very much to tap into them and bring about an overflow.

Lost Creativity

Due to lack of energy, enthusiasm or faith to apply our imaginations, creativity in ministry, in business or in life's labor diminishes. This builds fear for the future, thereby adding to the problem. Creative, artistic temperaments in particular need "down" time in which to recharge, time to allow the mind to work at its own pace, unbullied, until it naturally generates new and fresh ideas. When those ideas come bubbling to the surface, they bring with them a sense of relief, release and uplift that beats dozens of hours of counseling for the refreshment this release brings. Stage two burnout victims find their "down" time invaded and stolen while they feel powerless to stop it. As a result, anger and tension build up with no avenue for the creative release that would serve to release them.

Sexual Dysfunction

One's sex life may begin to suffer in stage two because the sufferer can no longer function adequately in the give and take of relationships, and because he is physically too weakened to generate much libido. This can exacerbate the stresses already present in the marriage, adding still more weight to the growing problem of burnout. Still, others may find tension release in *heightened* sexual activity or even in illicit aberrations like pornography or compulsive masturbation.

My wife, Beth, and I never stumbled in our marriage, but it became evident that in my withdrawal I failed to give her as much physical affection as I once had, either in public or in private. We had always enjoyed a happy marriage and she fully understood my condition, graciously granting me room to withdraw periodically as needed. At this point, however, one of the women in the church took it upon herself to decide how "hurt" Beth was and she attacked me for it. Beth corrected the misconception, but the incident played into all my other fears and stresses, thereby contributing to my downward spiral. Public figures will always be targets, but in this stage of burnout such shots cause more damage than they would otherwise.

Ministry to Stage Two

Torture! Now that they see the burnout victim falling into real trouble, friends and loved ones want to help, but rare indeed is the person who understands either the true nature of this suffering or what to do in response to it. Listen carefully to what follows.

Hold the Advice and Counsel

If approached at just the right moment and in just the right way, a burnout victim at this stage can still spill his hurt to another human being and receive ministry, but more than anything else he needs simply to be listened to with a sympathetic ear. He does not usually want a solution. In fact, unasked-for advice may lead to rage and even deeper withdrawal. No matter how good the advice may be, he knows in his heart that with his fading energies he cannot pursue it. He can therefore receive it only as more pressure to perform when he is rapidly losing the strength to perform. He really just needs a safe place to offload the pain until he can recover his strength or gather enough of himself together to remain functional a while longer.

He can still examine roots and causes for his pain in terms of his own hidden sins, but he can do so only at times of his own choosing. In Scripture Job's comforters come across as well-intentioned fools determined to convince him that his suffering resulted from something for which he needed to repent. They were wrong. Unfortunately the Body of Christ today abounds with Job's comforters. More than a few of them came to me in my pain to confront me "in love" and to show me that my plight stemmed from some hidden sin I needed to identify and confess. In truth sin always plays a role, but I could not have dealt with the sin issue at the time, and it was cruelty to demand that I do.

A Place for Fun

It may help a stage two burnout victim to kidnap him from time to time and take him out for fun of some kind, but refrain from talking business when you do. During this period in my life, a man who rarely darkened the door of our church used to show up on my doorstep on occasion and playfully ask my wife, "Can Loren come out and play?" He might have a trailer full of go-carts waiting out front, or a movie he wanted to see with a friend. One time he brought motorcycles, which I ride very poorly, but we had fun anyway. God arranged such healing times to restore my balance by rooting me in the good earth—and He used an ordinary friend to do it!

Discreet Prayer and Prophetic Input

Intercede in prayer, but mostly at a distance where your burnout victim feels no pressure to respond. He will sense your prayers. Tell him you are praying, but do not let him know very much of what you pray for. He can easily take this as pressure or responsibility to make your prayers happen, even though you would never intend them to be taken that way.

If the Lord gives you a specific Scripture reference or prophecy of hope for him, send it or give it in written form. It will feed his spirit. Do not confront him with it face-to-face. Rather leave him free to read it and to respond in private where he will feel no responsibility to you for his reaction.

Do not discuss his condition with others. If you do, he will likely sense it—or hear about it through the grapevine—and it will feed his growing paranoia. When you encounter others speaking about him in unclean or unedifying ways, stop them. Refuse even to answer questions from those who express a concern for him, except to say that he can always use prayer from those who love him.

Take Up the Sword

Take up the sword on his behalf. If your burnout victim is a pastor or leader, either in business or in the church, he will treasure above all your advocacy of his cause when there are battles to fight. I have valued few gifts more than the one the elders of the church I served in Idaho gave me when a fight erupted over changes we made to our bylaws to bring them more into conformity with the Scriptures. The reaction from a small but vocal minority was vicious and aimed at me personally. The opposition based their objections on distorted perceptions of what we had enacted, and they immediately turned to name-calling. They accused me of being everything from egomaniacal to cultish. In truth, after three years of warfare in which I had stood mostly alone, I teetered on the edge of collapse and lacked the strength to fight for my ego or create a cult even if I wanted to.

Up to that time, whenever the going got rough, my supporters and team lapsed into paralysis, left me to fight the battle alone and abandoned the flock to be devoured by wolves. This time the elders rallied and told me that it was their battle and not mine. That support brought more healing to me than anyone could imagine. As a result, the church came through in shining triumph, and God began to fulfill what He had promised for us.

4

STAGE THREE
BURNOUT—INCAPACITY

Of the three stages of wounding in burnout, this stands as the most misunderstood. In the mid-1980s I remained a part of the teaching team at Elijah House, the ministry my parents had founded a decade prior. I recall preparing for a seminar we had scheduled in which we planned to address burnout for the first time. Ultimately, the material we developed back then became the seed from which this book grew. As we met to prepare the teaching, we examined driving factors like performance orientation, the need for the wounded one to forgive betrayers and actions that could be taken to facilitate recovery. We talked at length about praying through the hurts that spring from betrayals until peace and resolution could be achieved. We looked at support systems and changes in lifestyle. It all sounded wonderful on the surface, but the longer we talked, the angrier I became. At first I could not fathom why.

Finally, it dawned on me that we were prescribing good medicine for someone in the earlier stages of burnout, but that same medicine would be dangerously destructive for the deeply wounded, among whom I had become a living example. The stage three burnout victim can no longer initiate or sustain his own recovery and therefore lives in a daily prison of despair. If we had pursued the course we were planning, we would have driven a number of those present at the seminar into deeper hopelessness because they would have come in a state of functional *incapacity*. Had we gone no further in our discussions, we would have been asking them to do what they had lost the ability to do. We would have failed—tragically—to address the needs of the incapacitated.

Some have been so deeply broken that they can only be carried, not exhorted and certainly not confronted. They must be loved, not instructed. Many of them have already prayed through all the things mentioned above as driving factors. They have examined and reexamined every root in sin they can think of or even imagine, and they have forgiven or repented for everything of which they are aware. It seems there remains nothing for them to try, and so they continue to hemorrhage emotionally. Experience has taught them that there exists no simple or quick means to the recovery they seek, and this knowledge fills them with fear.

Part of this despair stems from the fact that the Body of Christ seldom moves beyond a demand for simplistic and quick fixes. Especially in charismatic circles, which comprise a major share of my own beloved heritage, we have been taught and conditioned to seek instantaneous miracles. But there are no such miracles in store for third stage burnout victims, and they know it—a fact that deeply frightens them. Our simplistic solutions to their desperate problem serve only to drive them deeper into incapacity. Please give careful consideration to this section, even if some of it offends some personally cherished theological viewpoint. I know firsthand the truth of it.

Physical Symptoms

At some level third stage burnout victims feel ill every day, so worn out and physically and spiritually depleted that it seems their spirits have been installed in their bodies like a screw with the threads crossed. They feel slightly poisoned most of the time and suffer constant pain in various parts of their bodies. Adrenaline overproduction may have weakened their connective tissues so that they experience persistent aches and pains in various joints and ligaments.

The connective tissues in my shoulders used to hurt so badly that no amount of over-the-counter painkiller brought relief. Even my toe joints ached and occasionally spasmed. I had serious back problems and began seeing a chiropractor who complained that my ligaments had been so weakened that his adjustments would not hold.

For me, headaches became daily events, often arriving "on schedule" late in the afternoon and with such intensity that they occasionally caused nausea. Three to five painkiller tablets might deal with the discomfort, only to cause trembling due to overdose. Painful fluid-filled blisters appeared on the balls of my feet that had nothing to do with overuse or athlete's foot. As I later recovered from burnout, the blisters vanished.

Digestive disturbances become a daily struggle, every meal leading to later suffering. Food addictions, food allergies and food weaknesses can be greatly aggravated in this final stage. Paradoxically, my craving for sugar increased at the same time that I lost the physical ability to process it. For those in extremely stressful situations, refined sugar is a poison. Oh how I love sugar! But at this stage the aftermath of ingesting any sugar-laden delight devastated me. Healthy people often experience a "sugar high" followed by a letdown. I bypassed the high and went directly to the low, then felt as if a toxin were running through my system. The low made my eyes want to cross and I could barely stay awake. Sugar consumption sometimes brought on a headache.

Sleep is never satisfactory, provided it happens at all. Morning comes with a feeling of illness and people begin to comment on how bad the burnout victim looks.

At this point the victim's heart may begin to act up as a warning that he or she must do something quickly to correct their physical and emotional condition. Among those predisposed to heart disease, angina and heart attacks are not uncommon. I myself paid a visit to the family doctor because my heart was missing beats and convulsing, sometimes with pain. After running a series of tests, the doctor told me I was experiencing preventricular contractions. In other words, sometimes the ventricles of my heart failed to pump in proper sequence. I was in no immediate danger, but the warning could not be ignored. One young man I know began having false heart attacks, complete with the pain in his chest and arm consistent with a heart attack, even though his heart was healthy. Again, a warning!

The burnout victim experiences every other symptom listed under stages one and two, but in amplified form. Breakdown is imminent.

Emotional Condition

Unwelcome and out-of-control feelings will be the burnout victim's most devastating enemy. If those who tried to help in stage two missed it, here is where the truly hurtful mistakes can be made, especially by those who have not walked this way themselves. I pray this section provides some needed understanding for those who would come alongside.

Betrayed by God

Third stage burnout victims can find no respite from the sense that God has betrayed them. No divine promise can be trusted because God has broken them all and will neither help nor protect them. Without regard for their personal needs, God has utterly abandoned them. Although they may know in their heads that God loves them, they can find no place in their hearts to experience or believe it emotionally. These divine betrayals seem devastatingly real. Cognitive distortions have them trapped in a prison of darkness that blocks out all light and goodness from the world of reality.

For instance, in my daily devotions God might tell me to lengthen my tent cords and enlarge the place of meeting because He would be sending more growth to the church than we could house. The very next Sunday we would see a record low attendance for the year. God might promise me that my people would volunteer freely in the days of our power (reflecting a passage in the Psalms). There would be a workday on the church property scheduled for the following week and no one would show up. Did God really say these things? Whether or not He did, these things hit with a devastating thud.

It began to seem as though God were deliberately setting me up for disappointment just for the sake of torment. I no longer wanted to hear His voice, because each promise seemed like a setup for more heartache. My faith and trust were in tatters. Now, many years later, I see those promises coming true for the church I presently pastor, but in the midst of third stage burnout I had lost all perspective.

Prayer Life

Personal prayer life comes to a near standstill because it brings only pain. If burnout victims pray at all, they do so in settings where private intimacy with God is impossible. Ironically, they may continue to pray wonderfully in ministry situations because there they can still occasionally experience the presence and anointing of God flowing through for the sake of others, but they often feel betrayed afterward because the Lord seems not to be present for them personally.

Defenseless

Defenseless against the blows and pressures of daily life, every breakdown of routine, every failure of others to carry out their tasks as they overlap with the victim's brings on the deepest depression or even rage. Several times I stopped assigning tasks to others because I could no longer deal with the stress that resulted from feeling personally let down when others did not follow through. I could no longer risk the emotional devastation that resulted when my helpers failed me.

No resiliency remains, either emotionally or physically. Any exertion at all becomes extremely painful for every part of body and spirit. The burnout victim in stage three of degeneration feels like a fighter who can no longer ward off his opponent's blows. Unable even to hold up his fists, he can only resolve to remain in the ring and take it. Had the blows come with enough space between them, he could have caught his breath, cleared his head and remained on top of the fight, but too many pressures, crises and betrayals have piled one on top of another. He is finally broken.

Driven to Hatred

Backed into a corner until I had nothing left but rage, for the first time in my life I felt driven to active hatred of certain people in my church. Small, but effective, this group of persecutors caused all the more damage because of my fatigue and unresolved issues of rejection and fear.

For my love they returned criticism. For my best counsel they returned distorted reflections of all I had said, and, to make matters worse, they had enlisted others in the attack. They would declare, "He doesn't love us," while I stumbled around, exhausted from being there for them in their emergencies day after day in counsel, often into the wee hours of the morning. I recall spending half the night until 3:00 A.M. holding a barf bucket in the emergency room for one of our addicts, only to overhear her telling someone else,

"There's no love there." Because she was an addict, I should have been able to put that hurtful remark in perspective, but I could not.

The darkness and confusion this sick group of persecutors generated penetrated even the beauty of our worship and began to drag down the spirit of the entire congregation. Scarcely had the echoes of one incident died away before I would find myself facing another. Altogether it lacerated my spirituality and left me with the bitter taste of raw emotion in my mouth. I had never consciously hated anyone before and had thought myself incapable of it. In third stage burnout, I lost control and cried out to God, humbled and defeated, "I hate these people!"

Loss of Control

Every nerve burns. Without benefit of extraordinarily strong restraints built in early in life, those who have other-wise been kind and loving can suddenly become explosive, even violent, in their anger. Spouses of such wounded ones may be confused and hurt by volatile reactions to what seem to be small requests or insignificant irritants. Internally the wounded ones scream with rage and desperation. Gone are the physical resources that enable the mind to fight off insanity or overcome distorted perceptions.

I believe, but cannot substantiate, that the human body stores certain chemicals or nutrients as physical resources that it uses to combat stress. These enable us to maintain a grip on the whole of reality when particular aspects of real-ity become painful. Conditions of prolonged stress consume these resources at a faster rate than the body can effectively replace them. As a result, our spiritual, emotional and mental processes break down. Medical science provides very little help at this point because there seems to be no method for measuring these resources, much less an understanding of how to replenish them. The family doctor can only declare that his specific tests reveal no discernable physical or chemical abnormalities. Frustrated, sufferers know they are not hypochondriacs and that the physical and emotional pain they endure is real.

When we fought the battle in our church that I mentioned in the previous chapter (not the church I currently pastor), my reaction took me by surprise. Although suffering burnout symptoms, I had been feeling relatively good because the church had been at peace for an extended period of time. I believed I had recovered from the devastation of betrayals by friends and loved ones that I had suffered in the first few years after planting the church. I had not expected that a number of my family members (not my wife), most of whom were members of the church, would abandon me—or seem to—in my hour of greatest need. Some even led the opposition.

This abandonment lasted only about a week before most understood what I was actually trying to accomplish and took up my cause, but the damage had already been done. I had spent everything I had. There were no inner physical resources to draw upon. I felt as if a great, swirling black hole had opened up beneath me to suck me down into darkness. I remember thinking what a relief it would be just to give up and go completely crazy.

My mother-in-law, who lived with us at the time, had experienced two nervous breakdowns of her own. She overheard my wife and me discussing my symptoms, turned ashen white and began to pray, understanding the danger I faced in a way that few others could. She had lived a hard life, suffering the loss of her first husband to a divorce she never wanted. Post-Traumatic Stress Disorder (PTSD) cost her the father of my wife in the years following his service in World War II. After this came years of stress caring for her children on her own and finally marrying an emotionally abusive man. Stress took its toll until she found herself hospitalized for a time. Anyone suffering the effects of relentless stress without respite or relief can find her- or himself breaking apart in this way.

I took a vacation, demanding that I not be seen or contacted by anyone until I returned. Once I had disengaged, I held my own for a week or two before depression slammed into me once more. I saw my world disintegrating and could conceive of no pathway through the destruction I believed was coming. In the midst of it all, one of the elders of our church heard the call of the Spirit to come to my aid. He and his wife kidnapped my wife and me, taking us to a movie and then out for coffee afterward. It was the perfect moment. As they spoke positive reality to me concerning the condition of our church and the effectiveness of my ministry, my grip on reality began to be restored.

The believer who has reached this stage of wounding suffers frighteningly distorted perceptions of reality and nearly uncontrollable paranoia. Fear permeates every aspect of life. If he runs a business, revenues will dry up, trusted employees will resign and customers will abandon him. If he pastors, then offerings will be inadequate to maintain support, the church will lose members, key leaders will drop out and more. Who will be next in line to betray him? Whose tongue has been sowing criticism behind his back this time?

Past experience has taught him that no one will stand with him, and so he begins to mentally rehearse conflict situations in which he walks out or resigns. This includes angry speeches he wishes he could make in response to all of the assaults.

Inability to Receive

His inability to receive love and affection worsens, his heart so bruised that even the embrace of a safe family member causes pain. Emotional withdrawal seems now to be a near constant. Moments of vulnerability surface few and far between. A long time passed before I learned to kiss my wife again. In the depth of my wounding I could not tolerate anything or anyone "in my face" demanding a response— and in my cognitively distorted state of mind, "demand" was what it felt like. Simple offers of frontal affection irritated me at first, and then ignited sudden rage if my barriers were not respected.

Breakdowns in Ministry and Work

Demands for ministry at this point brought on extreme pain. The same would be true for anyone suffering a similar level of burnout in the secular world in a management position or other role of responsibility. I recall counseling sessions when the counselee had no idea that I was screaming inside, "Please! Make it stop!" as he or she poured out a litany of personal woe. The wounded one has nothing left to give. I learned to yawn with my mouth closed!

An extended vacation may help, but often serves only to make matters worse, as it did for me. In some cases, the wounded one may be so filled with anxiety concerning what might be going wrong at home that limited doses of contact with work may be necessary to keep him in touch with reality.

Vulnerability to Addictive Behavior

Resistance to all sorts of addictive behavior weakens at this stage. I worry that many burnout victims may be getting chemical help from their personal physicians at a time when dependency on drugs poses a real danger. Drugs often only suppress the problem, controlling feelings rather than resolving them, thus building up a debt to pay later. In my personal opinion, medicines should be taken only when no other means can be found to achieve sufficient clarity to allow real therapeutic discussion to occur in counseling. Drugs must never be seen as the solution. My personal physician and I agreed that even so innocent a drug as a sleeping pill would have been dangerous for me. I therefore resolved not to use them, but rather to find answers in my faith.

Rather than use drugs, I retreated into video games and became addicted to them, although they did nothing to relieve my stress. Anyone who has ever played a video game knows this to be a very tense way to have fun. I knew one burnout victim who became addicted to television and yet another who became a rude, idolatrous and obnoxious fanatic for televised sports. Others might turn to alcohol. The choices are as varied and numerous as the people who make them. Whatever the choice, addiction represents an attempt to medicate or block out feelings that have become unmanageable.

Suppressed Emotions

Continually suppressed emotions come back in distorted form. The burned-out believer has long been inadequately dealing with his feelings. I personally felt I had been forced to suppress mine. My upbringing programmed it and my experience in the church reinforced and confirmed it. If I shared my true feelings with anyone other than my wife, the shockwaves in the fellowship created more trouble than the temporary relief the sharing was worth.

Unfortunately, our society bears such a sickness in its attitude toward authority that any leader—in church, in business, in the home—who shares a weakness or a sin too openly, or in the wrong company, will certainly pay for it later. We search for faults in leaders and authority figures and then use our perception of them to tear down and weaken a leader's effectiveness. When no legitimate flaw can be dug up, we simply create one from nothing and then convince ourselves it is true. The wolves among the flock use the leader's weakness as a pretext to attack and accuse, while the weak and insecure find in it an excuse to spread poison among others who share their weakness. If the leader can be made to appear smaller, they can feel bigger in their smallness. They therefore welcome every opportunity to bring the leader down.

All of this multiplies the stress factors on the burnout victim so that the downward slide of the wounded one accelerates. I remember thinking bitterly that because of the ministry, I had neither the right nor the time to feel or display weakness of any kind.

Moral Vulnerability

Under normal conditions, morality is a settled gift in a strong man or woman of God. Temptations come, as they always do, but the exercise of a sanctified will routinely overcomes them. In deeply burned-out people, however, key strengths have sometimes been so catastrophically eroded that whatever cracks remain in their inner being, whatever areas of flesh or of sin that God has not been allowed to transform, may become gaping chasms under pressure. By means of natural strength and spiritual integrity they have controlled their sin nature in the past, but their capacity to continue has now been worn thin.

● Third stage burnout victims may therefore find themselves compulsively violating what they know to be clear, biblical moral imperatives. The following are confessions I have heard in counseling. Victims may be irresistibly drawn to pornography and be driven deeper into wounding by stress taking the form of shame and guilt. They may find themselves compulsively masturbating as a way of relieving emotional pressures. They may begin to think unexplainably violent thoughts and to visualize themselves doing violent things. They may find themselves drawn to men or women other than their spouses, especially if their behavior under stress has alienated their partner to some degree. Private drinking to excess can become a problem. Or it can be as seemingly inconsequential a thing as driving too fast too much of the time. All of this adds to the burden of guilt that aggravates their condition. Guilt and shame drive them ever more deeply into incapacity.

For those in ministry, confidence in personal anointing and ability to minister may be utterly destroyed to the degree that they begin to question their calling. People in business or leadership positions in the world at this stage often consider drastic actions like selling out and getting into a different line of work. This is largely due to a loss of perspective. In their weakened condition they can focus only on small things rather than the whole picture. Immediate and temporary problems seem permanent and insoluble when under normal circumstances their perception would be much more balanced.

It seems to them that their best efforts and most costly expenditures of energy have not produced fruit commensurate with the effort—certainly not enough to sustain their hope and purpose. They have given their best and have received scorn and criticism in return. If they counsel in their ministry they may have ignored that people take years to change, not days or months. They see every setback suffered by a counselee as a personal failure. They may speak of leaving the ministry, or even the church, and may hint at suicide. Take this latter threat seriously in most cases and do what you can to protect them from themselves. Better to be wrong and safe than wrong and wishing you had listened. Usually such talk is just catharsis, noise to be compassionately heard and then ignored, but you can never be certain. Apply this same dynamic of perceived failure and futility to a leader or worker in the world outside the church. The effect remains the same.

Ministry to Stage Three

Are you a helper? Are you feeling overwhelmed yet? If not, you probably should be—provided you have grasped the true depth of what is going on. The good news is that God has not left you powerless to help. Almost as important as what you *can* do is what you *must not* do, so please read carefully and empathetically.

Job's Comforters

Do not be a Job's comforter. At this depth of devastation, avoid confronting the wounded one with the bitter root judgments and sins that may have set him up for this problem. At this point he cannot engage in that kind of introspection or deal constructively with the healing process associated with it. To do so requires inner resources and strength he no longer possesses. Often, he has already crucified himself with self-examination and has come up empty-handed, having discovered nothing to account for his condition. Seeking a way out of the pain, he has probably repented in every way he knows how and, like Job, he may have realized by now that the suffering under which he labors will not be alleviated by repentance for some mysterious hidden sin.

In short, this is not the time for corrective ministry. "Nouthetic" (confrontive) counseling may serve only to drive him over the edge. Corrective ministry becomes possible only after liberal doses of compassion and some recovery of strength. Do not analyze the roots of the problem at this stage unless he asks for it, and then do so very carefully and sparingly.

Do Not Do Deliverance Ministry

In most cases, deliverance ministry is a foolish approach. Spirits of oppression are *not* the source of the burnout's problem. He will not get better as a result of your prayers for deliverance and will only feel more betrayed by God for the failure of your efforts to change anything. Demonic influence may be contributing to the problem, but the root lies elsewhere. If you must cast demons off of or out of him, do so where he cannot hear you doing it.

Do Not Preach God's Love

I know this may sound odd and even heretical, but it can cause more harm than good to tell the wounded one that God loves him. As a believer he already understands that theology. At an emotional level, however, he cannot believe that God loves him and is convinced that the evidence points to the absence of that love. Your affirmation of it only brings him face-to-face with his pain in that regard and sharpens his sense of deficit.

Tell him that *you* love him. He may not believe it, but your words and your presence will seem more real to him than the love of a God he can neither see nor any longer feel. It will then be your responsibility to prove that you mean what you say by not failing or betraying him.

Do Not Announce What You See Being Purified

You may feel drawn to point out what inner imperfections you believe you see God burning out of his nature, or to piously affirm that this is, after all, a sanctifying, purifying experience sent or used by God to "get the 'gunk' out." While it may be true that God is, in fact, using the situation to accomplish such a cleansing, to the wounded one God is a betrayer and he has had enough of pain. Paradoxically, he already instinctively knows that what you say is true. If he did not, he would be long gone already.

Respect Fences

Up to a point, respect his fences and his withdrawal. Be secure enough in yourself not to take these things as a rejection of you personally. He simply can no longer respond normally to others and, if pushed to do so, the result may be an explosion of rage, followed by a deeper flight from relationships. Do not demand that he talk to you or that he listen to your advice. Allow him to choose the times of sharing on his own and let him determine how deep the sharing goes. Never push or pry.

Time Management

Avoid talking "time management." Seldom, if ever, is this truly the problem. For the third stage burnout victim, management of time feels like just another thing to do, something to work at, and he cannot absorb any more of that. The same is true of counseling him to delegate more of his work. Those he depended on have let him down too many times. Trusted lieutenants have not followed through in their tasks and he can no longer risk being wounded by their ongoing failures. If you truly wish to lift some of the burden, just *do* it and then tell him afterward.

Harmful Religious Advice

Telling someone to praise God *for* all things (see Ephesians 5:20) can be wonderful biblical counsel for a healthy sufferer, but it places a cruel burden on an incapacitated wounded servant. He *cannot* do it. His best approach to God is an honest cry of rage. At this point in my life I had nothing left to offer God emotionally than complete honesty concerning how I felt. As I expressed my anger to Him and at Him, I knew I still had a relationship with Him. Better anger than no communication at all! I called Him every name in the book, both fair and foul, and found Him big enough not to be offended by it as I got it off my chest.

As with a stage two sufferer, refrain from delivering face-to-face prophecies that must be responded to, no matter how encouraging their content may seem to be. Such prophecies come across as sandpaper on an open wound. Write them out and send them by mail or email, or deliver them by hand with the understanding that they can be read later, privately, where no perception of demand for response can intrude.

Pray for a stage three burnout victim at a respectful distance. Tell him that you are praying and that you care deeply but leave it at that. If you let him know the specific content of your prayers, he will feel a responsibility to do something about it, which is a burden he does not need. If you simply assure him that you are praying and that you care, he will receive encouragement without feeling any pressure to respond.

Love without Demand

Love him in ways that demand no response. Whether family or friend, do not "get in his face" with frontal hugs or penetrating eye contact. Many wounded ones absolutely cannot bear the intensity of full-frontal interaction, so let hugs be sideways or from behind and do not demand eye contact. Let expressions of love take the form of a touch on the hand or an affectionate poke in the ribs.

Listen. Be available. The rare moment of vulnerability may surface at any time. I used to talk to my wife in bed, late at night, often rudely rousing her from a sound sleep. Under any other circumstances, this would be considered the height of insensitivity, but I really could not help it. I knew that if I allowed the moment to pass, I would not be able to manufacture it later—or even remember what I wanted to say. More than anyone else she understood that I did not want answers to my sharing, that it was enough for me just to be able to express myself to one who would not be dragged down by my gloomy outlook.

Believe in your sufferer and let him know that you do. My wife assured me over and over again that I was a good father and a good pastor, because I believed I had failed at everything. See and affirm your wounded one's gifts and determine not to waver in your faith for him.

At the appropriate time, pursue the wounded one and speak truth to him concerning what is right and good in his ministry, his work and his life. Time this carefully under the guidance of the Holy Spirit because, if approached at the wrong time or in the wrong way, the wounded one can be driven further into withdrawal. A good illustration is the story I told earlier about one of the elders of my church who came to me at the bottom of my despair and spoke loving truth to me. The third stage burnout victim is in danger of losing his grip on reality. Withdrawal forms a perceptual prison that locks out any correctives to a fatal loss of perspective. Without those correctives, the nightmare of despair can become both bottomless and endless.

Send encouraging gifts and cards of love and appreciation for what the wounded one has given to you, but remember not to demand any sort of response.

5

PERSONAL SURVIVAL—WHAT THE WOUNDED ONE CAN DO

At that first seminar on burnout that the Elijah House team and I taught in Spokane, Washington, all those years ago, someone asked how I survived my own experience. My multi-faceted answer began with praise for my wife who instinctively did for me what needed to be done. At a crucial point in my walk through that wilderness, a friend tracked me down and spoke the truth to me in a way that I could hear and respond to. At the Lord's urging, others sent me encouragement in the mail or delivered written prophecies by hand that I could read later. But by and large, most people did all the wrong things. I come from parents who occupy the top rung of the ladder among Christian counselors in this country, and even they did all the wrong things!

This chapter includes a number of survival decisions and skills you will need should the Lord choose to move you further down the road to refinement and plunge you into the dark night of the soul. I regard my years of burnout as a time when God taught me much of what I needed to know to successfully navigate the shoals of those dark waters. I could therefore pass through that deeper wilderness having already made the most crucial decisions.

The Gift of Mental Discipline

By grace, somewhere in the course of my life, the most important thing God gave me was the gift of mental discipline. Part of it came from the training I received as a child when my parents refused to allow me to act out my negative emotions in ways that might harm others. That training formed a second-nature restraint that I could rely upon without having to work very hard at it. With a good foundation in both physical affection and discipline I could face the most severe tests choosing to know what I needed to know well enough to survive.

I realize that many of us were not given this training as children. Without it, the battle for control and survival becomes immeasurably more difficult, but remains winnable. In the mid-1980s I worked with one young pastor in the depths of wounding who lost control and became abusive with his wife and son for a time. Walls of restraint had not been built into his character during his early life and so he broke under the pressure of the crisis he faced. In the first years of his ministry and then in the early stages of burnout, he maintained a kind and gentle demeanor through the discipline of prayer and a determination to pursue his Christian walk with integrity.

What came out of him later horrified him. He exploded, becoming verbally and even physically violent with his family, then fought with all his failing strength to regain his discipline. He struggled. He wept. He despaired. In the depths of desperation he actually considered divorcing his wife so as to remove any opportunity to abuse her again. He pled for the Lord's discipline and sought wise and compassionate counsel. In the end, the Lord Himself provided for him the discipline he lacked. God became his Father. Therefore, although it can be more difficult for those not trained in it, discipline remains possible. The war can be won.

In the depths of my own wounding, I disciplined myself to weigh the consequences of losing control against the pain of hanging on, and therefore refused to surrender to insanity. I knew that every time I acted on my anger, I would only create more stress for myself than I was already suffering. I reasoned that most people could never understand and would only be hurt by my outbursts. In the end, matters would be worse. If I turned to accusation of others as a means of alleviating inner pressures, I would only drive people to defend themselves by attacking me.

When I considered leaving the ministry, I clung to the knowledge that if I couldn't make it at the church I served at the time, there was no place else for me to go. My integrity would forever be in question, even in my own eyes. Rather than quit, I faithfully pastored that congregation until I knew that I had accomplished what God had called me to accomplish.

I made myself account for what my children would lose if I allowed myself to fall apart. Because I knew that the pain I would suffer for taking their heritage from them would be worse than the pain I was already experiencing, I refused to let go of my faith. I chose to stand and I forced myself to do it. No matter what, I *decided* to believe.

Principles of Survival

Many years ago I tried bodysurfing off the California coast. It must have been due to brain damage, because I am no kind of swimmer. I sink like a rock. Surprisingly, however, I caught the first wave just right and experienced a wonderful sensation almost like flying, with my upper body projected out of the water as the wave stretched out below me.

The second wave did not work out so well. I missed the sweet spot and found myself hyperventilating, frantically treading water and unable to pull myself up and into a position where I could swim out of the trouble I found myself in. Panic took over, which only made the situation worse. Paralyzed by fear, I could not think of what to do. Had a friend not saved me, I would have drowned that day.

Many of us in deep burnout feel just like that. Drowning and overcome by fears we do not understand, we cannot think of how to swim out. In the pages that follow, reach deep into your inner strength and try to do what I tell you that you must do. It may save your life.

Know What You Know

The first principle of survival is therefore to *know what you know for the sake of others who depend on you.* You may not always succeed in this most important discipline, but the effort alone may enable you to survive.

At the depth of burnout I learned that feelings simply exist. By themselves they are morally neutral. As extensions of our sinful flesh they are at least forgivable. In our helplessness to control those feelings that fail to line up with God's nature, our only hope for victory is to confess our helplessness and receive the Lord's mercy. Feelings do not necessarily have substance, nor do they necessarily reflect reality. As such they cannot be relied upon to shape decisions in the real world. Feelings play an essential role in our lives, but that role does not include making decisions for action. Roughly analogous to the nervous system in the physical body, feelings inform us when something has gone wrong by sending a pain message, or when something good is happening by sending a pleasure message—but their function ends there.

I therefore survived, in part, by learning to separate what I felt inwardly from what I did outwardly. I learned that what is right to do, or true to believe, often has little or nothing to do with what I feel. I can experience an emotion in one part of myself while doing the opposite of that feeling in another part of myself just because the doing represents objectively righteous action. Unfortunately, burned out or not, most of us stumble through life acting out our subjectivities, living as victims driven by our emotions and consistently reaping trouble for it. "The heart is more deceitful than all else and is desperately sick; who can understand it?" (Jeremiah 17:9).

Living from a base in feelings may be fine when feelings coincide with objective reality or with God's own righteousness, but every one of us must somehow learn to do the right thing when our emotions lead in a different direction. Know what you know, and insofar as your incapacity at the depth of burnout will allow, *do* what you know. You may not succeed. You may be too "wasted" to succeed. But the effort may keep you sane, protect your loved ones and train into you an inner discipline that will yield huge dividends later.

Embrace the Fireball

The second principle of survival is to "embrace the fireball." I took that phrase from a dream a young college student once asked me to interpret. In the dream the Lord Jesus appeared and handed him a ball of fire the size of a basketball. Jesus instructed him to hug it to himself. As he obeyed he suffered excruciating pain, but embedded in the pain was something terribly good. I knew that the Lord was about to plunge him into some kind of trial intended to purify his heart and that he must embrace the experience rather than fight it.

First Peter 4:1 calls us to prepare for this: "Therefore, since Christ has suffered in the flesh, arm yourselves also with the same purpose, because he who has suffered in the flesh has ceased from sin." Similarly, verses 12–13 exhort, "Beloved, do not be surprised at the fiery ordeal among you, which comes upon you for your testing, as though some strange thing were happening to you; but to the degree that you share the sufferings of Christ, keep on rejoicing, so that also at the revelation of His glory you may rejoice with exultation."

Although I could not tolerate others pointing out that God intended my experience to produce sanctification, I knew the truth of it. From the mouths of others, however, it sounded like pious sermons from people whose ignorance bordered on cruelty. I even knew that the hurt I felt resulted from no specific wrongdoing, at least not any I could see at the time. I had a task to perform for the Lord, a life calling, and for that task, my personality, my gifts, my abilities and even my way of meeting life had to be honed, refined and changed. As the old saying goes, "You can't get there from here."

At times when the suffering just seemed senseless I lost touch with this basic knowledge, but on the whole it contributed to my continuing grip on sanity. I learned that the difference between redemptive suffering and destructive misery lies in the degree to which one fights, rather than accepts, the pain. I found a peculiar measure of peace in surrendering to it and embracing it, even though I often felt rage and frustration. Although not constant in that peace, I survived and was certainly changed. Much more would come with the dark night of the soul.

Job determined, "Though He slay me, I will hope in Him" (Job 13:15). He went on to protest his innocence and carried on a lengthy argument with God, but in the end, when the Lord revealed Himself, he admitted: "I have heard of You by the hearing of the ear; but now my eye sees You; therefore I retract, and I repent in dust and ashes" (Job 42:5–6).

Job did not and could not describe what he had learned. Even now, I myself would have difficulty describing the changes in my character and in my relationship with God, but people who have known me through the years certainly notice it. People hear me in ways they never did in the years before burnout and the dark night of the soul had burned through me. I deal with crises more effectively and with a greater measure of security. I have become a better leader and a more whole family man. I learned the hard way that knowledge comes from study, but wisdom comes only through suffering. I have therefore determined to welcome suffering and have developed a fresh understanding of what the Preacher meant when he wrote: "Sorrow is better than laughter, for when a face is sad a heart may be happy. The mind of the wise is in the house of mourning, while the mind of fools is in the house of pleasure" (Ecclesiastes 7:3–4). 4/26/16 - See John Thomas·

Learn to Love Obedience

I used to love serving the Lord for the fruit I saw in my ministry. Producing for God can be a lot of fun, but then He took away my ability to produce by sending a swarm of locusts to eat up all my fruit. I had to learn to obey whether I saw fruit from my labor or not. I had to come to a point at which it would be enough for me emotionally just to know that I had done what God had asked me to do. I began to teach others that obedience to the Lord must be its own reward—whether in business, ministry or life.

Share in a Safe Environment

Find a safe place to "dump" your feelings. Do it on a regular basis and as an act of obedience to God. It may not be easy but it is certainly necessary. James 5:16, much neglected by Protestants today, commands us: "Therefore, confess your sins to one another, and pray for one another so that you may be healed."

During my burnout years in the 1980s in north Idaho, my dumping place was our elders' group that met weekly with our wives. These men and women partnered with me in ministry and we had developed a trust relationship in spite of the many ways in which we had failed one another. For a season, I made it a weekly discipline to report to them on my emotional state. They needed to know, and I needed to objectify what I felt by sharing it. At times, I wanted to hide, but I worked against the impulse because I knew it spelled the difference between recovery and failure.

Learn Not to Share with Those Who Wound

Sensing your condition, a surprising number of well-intentioned church people will be eager to express deepest concern and love for you, but not all are safe. These people appear in many forms and may be of either gender. "I would never hurt you," they promise. "Please tell me if I ever do." Do not believe it!

Because of the need to protect certain people, I have put together the following story as a composite of many stories. Most, but not all, of the wounders who have crossed my path have been seriously broken people with a need to gain some kind of control over authority figures and others in their lives. Obviously this kind of problem can involve both men and women, but women seem more susceptible to the kind of thing I am about to describe. I realize that I may suffer some abuse for such a statement in our increasingly feminist culture, but this accurately reflects my experience.

This sort of woman "gentles" her way into the life of a male leader in emotional trouble until, in some weak moment of vulnerability, off guard and feeling leaky, he spills a portion of his pain. This part of the story often unfolds in a secular office situation where the burned-out leader or boss associates with female employees of a makeup similar to the one I have outlined.

In a church setting, because these women tend to congregate with other women who share similar backgrounds of childhood abuse, a whole group of them will shortly be discussing the content of what the male leader leaked. They will share this grave "concern" among themselves and pray up a storm, fanning the flames of their emotions and becoming more and more deluded. They do not believe anything they are doing is wrong because, after all, these women they share with are their friends. In their opinion, they share only to submit their burdens and perceptions to trusted others for confirmation and balance. They may express these concerns to their husbands, as well, so that, unless a man is exceptionally strong, he falls into the negative talk and the delusionary thinking along with his wife.

Before long, the group arrives at a solution for, or analysis of, the leader's problem and they want to minister to it. Their analysis and solution fall well wide of the mark and almost always come across as a set of accusations. Of course, they offer these "in love" while they cut the leader to the very heart. Worse, when he rejects their "prophetic words" because of their inaccuracy, they accuse him of being one who does not listen and who cannot receive correction. This sets off a round of new criticism and even more negative talk.

Understand that these well-intentioned saints of the Lord act with no awareness of the true nature or consequences of their actions. Love them, but avoid sharing with them anything of substance from your own heart.

DEWS—the Distant Early Warning System

I know of no better way to identify wounders and to avoid falling into their traps than to listen to the Distant Early Warning System that God has placed in our spouses. God has endowed them with a failsafe sense of when something or someone poses a threat to us, and we do well to heed it. My emotionally whole and balanced wife has unfailingly spotted such approaching threats and has warned me ahead of time. I learned the hard way to listen to her by suffering the situation I described above on more than one occasion. I no longer ignore or discount her warnings. Ever.

If you struggle with third stage burnout without benefit of a spouse, or if your mate suffers the same level of burnout as you do, then seek out reliable prophetic people in your flock, fellowship or workplace who can see the sin in the hearts of people and warn you concerning impending danger. Then heed them for your own sake and for the sake of those you lead or affect.

Feed Your Weakened Spirit

Feed your weakened spirit in ways that require minimal expenditure of energy. Begin by cleansing your mind and heart of standard Christian religious ideas concerning how to get refreshment from the Lord and then prepare yourself for something that may be different for you. Standard Christian piety works well under normal conditions, but for deeply wounded ones it often presents demands that can no longer be met. In His grace, God can refresh, instruct and correct His servants through a multitude of unlikely means. Remember that He spoke to Balaam by the mouth of a donkey. Sometimes we need to be surprised, even ambushed, by our Father when the old and familiar has lost its capacity to impact us. After such an ambush, the old and familiar takes on new life, having been infused with a new ability to touch us.

Try listening to good music, both secular and sacred. Refuse to listen to those who say that Christians should listen only to Christian music. At one point in my own process of recovery I dug out some old Joni Mitchell records from my "hippie" days. She wrote marvelous lyrics set to deeply melancholic melodies with an ever-present reminder of a simpler life. Sometimes she sang in such a beautiful way of such dismal hopelessness that if the music were not so beautiful, the listener would be crushed. Locked up emotionally, I found her songs expressed something of what I held inside. The music connected with what I felt and released imprisoned emotions. On numerous occasions I sat before the stereo and wept.

I watched movies like the Rocky series, in which a nobody from a Philadelphia slum fought his way to the top of the boxing world, suffered defeat and then fought his way back again. Along the way, he found his true self, learned to pray and became a family man. I own that complete set on video.

The Star Wars and Star Trek series both spoke to me, and I have no patience with the religious spirit that criticizes them for not holding to a biblical theology. They painted an imaginary world, after all, and made no pretense of reality. These series, as well, made their way into my video library. I will never forget Yoda, the Jedi master, instructing Luke Skywalker, his student, "Judge you me by my size? The Force is my ally, and a powerful ally it is," as he prepared Luke to achieve victory against overwhelming odds.

Both series told stories of people who snatched victory from the jaws of defeat and who came from behind to overcome overwhelmingly powerful enemies, often with supernatural help. It did not matter to me that the Force of *Star Wars* is not the God of the Bible. The point was that all those little people overcame enormous opposition with the help of their god as they understood him—or "it" as the Force would be more properly referenced.

I reread J. R. R. Tolkien's *The Lord of the Rings* and a whole group of other fantasies by Christian and non-Christian authors alike. I desperately needed a fresh injection of imagination and magic (in its good and figurative sense) in my life to renew my dying sense of the supernatural. God gave a measure of that renewal to me through some of the world's great literature and media.

Through all such stories runs a common theme—recovery of power after a crushing defeat by an enemy who seems invincible. These tales and others like them tell of little men doing great things in the face of overwhelming odds. They include lessons on the misuse of power and on the strength to be found in weakness. They reminded me that I am a winner by nature and by anointing and that I have a great God on my side. I had not lost the war, but the cost of fighting had left me so weak and broken that I had forgotten what strength felt like.

These simple movies and wonderful books rekindled a dying flame and sent me soaring. God met me there. It does not bother me that many of them present a non-Christian worldview. We do not need to be afraid of that sort of thing. For most of us reading these words right now, a lifetime of commitment to the Lord's Word automatically separates pollution from truth. Out of their pagan settings God lifted valuable insights that I needed to hear and made them shine for me.

To date, I have read Tolkien at least five times. I own the movies and have practically memorized the dialog. I have seen each of the Rocky movies more times than I can count. Later on, I added *Braveheart* to the collection. Religious readers might think me seriously deluded for all of this, but I stated at the beginning that I did not write this book to spark a debate. Think what you like; I know what I know. God used those secular sources to revitalize the reading of His Word for me and, as a result, I saw things in the Scriptures that I had not seen before. The Bible held new encouragement for me as God refreshed me by means of unlikely springs. Watch Luke Skywalker battle the evil Darth Vader, or Rocky defeat the powerful Russian who killed his friend in the ring, then open your Bible and read of David as he faced Goliath, or of Moses standing before great Pharaoh and you will know what I mean.

Others might find inspiration in the heroic stories of King Arthur or Robin Hood. Still others might be drawn to works of great classical music or poetry. Time spent in the vastness of nature might recall greatness and rekindle imagination concerning the wonder and power of God. Jesus Himself frequently retreated to the mountaintop or to a lonely place to pray.

In short, nourish your spirit on great music, great poetry, heroic stories and films, or whatever else reignites your dying flame, and do not limit the kinds of vehicles God can use to do that. All true beauty and truth come from Him. Whatever you consume, let it stand under the judgment of the eternal Word, the Bible. All good wine must be cleansed by passing through that True Filter.

Get Someone to "Lie" for You

Really! Stay with me, now! You need to establish forms of protection for yourself that others—not you—bear responsibility to maintain. My wife and my secretary do this for me even today. When they see that I have become too tired, they very sweetly and professionally keep people away and I do not ask them to check with me when they do. They often know better than I when I should not be saying yes.

During the burnout years in north Idaho, my wife and my mother-in-law, who lived with us at the time, took care of that boundary. We had the church phone wired to ring both at the church facility and at our home—and I learned never to answer it myself. Here's the "lying" part! Clever enough to tell selective truths about my availability, my wife told callers only what they really had to know so that they hung up the phone understanding that I could not be reached, but without feeling rejected. My mother-in-law, on the other hand, could not think as quickly as my wife and might therefore tell callers I was not at home when, in fact, I was. A sanctified lie!

Understand my point. In recovering from burnout there must be times when you surrender the right to decide when you have spent too much of yourself. You have probably never been good at saying no when you need to. I myself have become better at it through the years, but it is a big jump from "better" to "good."

Still worried about that "lying" part? In Joshua 2 Rahab the harlot lied to the defenders of Jericho to protect the spies sent from Joshua to spy out the city. In Judges 4 Jael deceived

Sisera to kill him for the sake of the people of Israel. Both women received praise and reward for their acts and stand today as heroines of the faith. 'Nuff said? Make a place, albeit a small and cautious one, for sanctified lying when you need to protect your strength and there seems to be no other way. And let someone else do it.

Do Not Assume Guilt or a Character Flaw

Never automatically assume that the cause of your burnout must be personal sin or a character flaw. Although sin or character flaws may indeed be involved, that kind of self-examination will not be helpful at the depth of your wounding. Job suffered terribly, but not as a result of any of the usual personal shortcomings we might expect or look for. Although clear unrighteousness on Job's part did not cause his suffering, the experience profoundly changed both him and his relationship with God. More on this in a later chapter! For now, suffice it to say that the same transformation will be yours if you but seek to stand your ground in faith and wait it out.

When You Cannot Praise God, Be Honest

Pour out your pain to God. Call Him names if you have to. Far from being offended, He will probably fall off His throne laughing. Compassionately! Suppression of emotion brings a terrible reaping while open honesty cleanses. In my deepest rage and despair I even swore at Him. I discovered He does not have virgin ears and that His presence is the one safe place in all the world where I can be whatever I happen to be at the moment in perfect safety. Besides, does He not already know the content of my heart! Better to hurl my honest rage and accusation at my Lord and Savior than not to pray at all. The most cursory reading of the Psalms reveals more than ample scriptural precedent for expressing personal feelings before God in this way.

Do Not Quit

If the obstacles you face seem too overwhelming, at least refuse to quit. In this refusal you ensure victory. The great spiritual warfare passage, Ephesians 6:10–17, most strongly emphasizes "standing firm." God does not require us to conquer or personally defeat the spiritual hosts of wickedness. Nor is it necessary that you function at full capacity in your effort to stand firm. You need only refuse to move.

First, by your refusal to move, you give God room to work the sort of transformation in your heart that He made in Job's heart. Often those who flee the scene of suffering only remove themselves from the fire of God set to test them and so cheat themselves of the strength and wisdom that develop only in the heat of tribulation and death.

Second, as you stand firm you break the heart of your enemy, whether that enemy is a spiritual force, a situation or a person. I once told a troublemaker, "I'm tougher than anyone here and I'll be here long after you're gone." Never mind that my words failed to reflect my inner feelings. Her whole crowd was soon history while I reaped years of abundance. Your adversary, the devil, occupies an even worse position than your human opponent. You have eternity in which to stand. He does not. God has appointed the time of his doom and limited the season of his freedom to move. You may be so broken that you can no longer fight, but you can at least refuse to get out of the ring.

Know Your Innocence

Often your burnout results from a barrage of accusations leveled at you by those you lead and for whom you have poured forth your best gifts of love and service. Because you know the mistakes you have made, you may try to wear those accusations. Somehow you feel that if you could just do everything right, they would all love you for it, and because that love is not forthcoming, you feel it must be your fault.

Foolishness! There comes a time when you must call a halt to self-examination and introspection and take stock of your integrity. Claim your innocence. The time came when I had to say, "I have not done that of which you accuse me! I have not manipulated. I never said what you insist that I said. I did not mean what you chose to believe I meant. I did not betray to others what you shared with me in confidence; it was you, yourself, who leaked the information and it was those trusted friends of yours that you leaked it to who passed it around!"

I think you get the idea. Although I never made a claim to perfection, I had not sinned against these people—at least not in the ways they thought I had. I had to be driven to the point of rage before I could take this stand. Up until that point I had nearly destroyed myself with misplaced guilt, doubts and questions.

Whether in the church or in the world, those of us with pastors' hearts have a very difficult time accepting the fact that people are basically nasty. We want to believe in them, and we would rather blame ourselves than face the possibility that the heart of a loved one might be as black as night and set on destruction.

Get Mad

Pray the "bloody" psalms. God will know what to do with them, even if, in your rage, you intend more than could be considered righteous. Do this not to wish evil on your enemies, but as a kind of catharsis before God. Get the hurt out of your system. Pour it out to God by means of the words of Scripture. Praying in this way will provide you a form of holy release, while loosing spiritual power to defeat your enemies.

I must qualify this by saying that what might have been acceptable during my burnout years was not permissible later in the dark night of the soul. In the dark night of the soul,

God dealt with my anger and held me, as He still does, to a strict regime of praying genuine blessing on my enemies. Jesus said, "Love your enemies," but during the burnout years it helped to pray these disturbingly violent psalms. Examples follow:

> Contend, O LORD, with those who contend with me;
> Fight against those who fight against me.
> Take hold of buckler and shield
> And rise up for my help.
> Draw also the spear and the battle-axe to meet those
>   who pursue me;
> Say to my soul, "I am your salvation."
> Let those be ashamed and dishonored who seek my
>   life;
> Let those be turned back and humiliated who devise
>   evil against me.
> Let them be like chaff before the wind,
> With the angel of the LORD driving them on.
> Let their way be dark and slippery,
> With the angel of the LORD pursuing them.
> For without cause they hid their net for me;
> Without cause they dug a pit for my soul.
> Let destruction come upon him unawares,
> And let the net which he hid catch himself;
> Into that very destruction let him fall.
>
> Psalm 35:1–8

> O God, shatter their teeth in their mouth;
> Break out the fangs of the young lions, O LORD.
> Let them flow away like water that runs off;
> When he aims his arrows, let them be as headless
>   shafts.
>
> Psalm 58:6–7

> May their eyes grow dim so that they cannot see,
> And make their loins shake continually.
> Pour out Your indignation on them,

And may Your burning anger overtake them.
May their camp be desolate;
    May none dwell in their tents.
For they have persecuted him whom You Yourself
    have smitten,
    And they tell of the pain of those whom You have
    wounded.
Add iniquity to their iniquity,
    And may they not come into Your righteousness.
May they be blotted out of the book of life
    And may they not be recorded with the righteous.

Psalm 69:23–28

Appoint a wicked man over him,
    And let an accuser stand at his right hand.
When he is judged, let him come forth guilty,
    And let his prayer become sin.
Let his days be few;
    Let another take his office.
Let his children be fatherless
    And his wife a widow.
Let his children wander about and beg;
    And let them seek sustenance far from their ruined
    homes.
Let the creditor seize all that he has,
    And let strangers plunder the product of his labor.
Let there be none to extend lovingkindness to him,
    Nor any to be gracious to his fatherless children.
Let his posterity be cut off;
    In a following generation let their name be blotted
    out.

Psalm 109:6–13

Ultimately, God publicly shamed each of those who falsely accused and persecuted me during the burnout years. While I did next to nothing, He sovereignly revealed their sin before the whole flock until with one voice the fellowship cried, "Enough!"

When the judgment of God falls on such people the purpose is redemptive, but when they reap the Law, full grown, devastation results. The judgment of a loving God restores the repentant heart, while the reaping of the Law simply destroys. "God is not mocked; for whatever a man sows, this he will also reap" (Galatians 6:7). Therefore, in the mystery of God, I believe such bloody prayers actually seek God's mercy, desiring that His judgment, rather than the reaping of the Law, would come to those who have done such damage.

Unfortunately, most of those who caused me all that pain could never find it in their hearts to repent. As I followed their histories in the years after they left us, I discovered a consistent pattern of disaster in the form of bankruptcies, incest, family breakups and house fires, to name but a few. As the author of Hebrews wrote: "It is a terrifying thing to fall into the hands of the living God" (10:31).

Nevertheless, if any of these people ever appeared at my door needing help, I would give it. Without evidence of real repentance and change, one or two would not be allowed back into any flock I might pastor, but all would be welcome to my personal ministry.

6

BREAKING DESTRUCTIVE LIFE PATTERNS

Held captive to what they do, burnout victims often sacrifice self and health well beyond any valid call of God. I recall thinking—and rightly so—that my life and faith should be a model for others. Late in the burnout years I found myself questioning, "But where is my joy? Would I invite others into this pain I feel? Is the Christian walk an invitation to constant fatigue? Do I really want others to become as unbalanced as I am? Looking at the quality of my life, why would anyone want to join me in my faith?" At that point my recovery from burnout and the rediscovery of joy became issues of personal integrity. How could I preach the peace of God when I had so little of it myself?

Breaking the Personal Obligation Pattern

Most burnout victims in ministry or in other forms of leadership feel personally obligated to everyone in their care. This can be motivated by fear of not being liked for saying no once in a while. Or victims may genuinely believe that without their direct involvement terrible things will happen in the lives of those who look to them for leadership. This can happen to those at the top of the corporate ladder and it can afflict those who hold no higher position than head of a household. Those afflicted by the personal obligation pattern have an overblown sense of their own responsibility and too little faith in Jesus' ability to take care of people and situations.

They may own the failures of others in their sphere of influence and therefore cannot risk allowing them to fail. In short, they cannot withdraw from perceived obligations often enough or long enough to remain healthy. Locked into this sense of personal responsibility, and imprisoned by their inability to say no, they cannot even permit others to say no on their behalf.

I began to learn to say no when I began to experience such anger with the escalating demands of selfishly "sick" people in the church I pastored, and when I became so frustrated with my own condition, that extreme discomfort drove me to action. After all these years, I remain a bit dysfunctional in this area, but I work at overcoming it. For instance, the telephone rings and it is Melvin calling again with the same story he tells again and again, with the same pain, again and again. I am not at home, but my wife promises that I will return his call. I do not. Angrily I do not. Feels good, too! And amazingly, Melvin survives! You may not need the anger to do the right thing, but if you need it, use it!

The building committee has chosen to meet on my day off. I know they will make decisions concerning the shape of our new building that I will hate later. My pastoral perspective (translate "control") is needed. The chairman knew better than to schedule the meeting for that day, darn his hide! Well, I am not coming! Take that! Talked to the architect two days later. Corrected some errors. Everybody lived.

Planning our vacation. Gosh, I need it this year! But family expects us to visit. Aunt Maimie will be there. She has been judging me for fifteen years and she will be doing it again.

Nothing will be said to my face, but I will feel it in the air and her husband will hear about it later. I cannot deal with it this year. I need this vacation away from the stress of constantly juggling other people's feelings, but with her around, I will not get it. The family will be upset if we do not come? Good! I will not be there to see it! Now, where else can we go to be alone?

Breaking the Self-sacrifice Pattern

I make self-sacrifice a major cornerstone of my preaching. I believe that a focus on self leads directly to depression and a shipwreck of a life. On the other hand, some forms of self-sacrifice and our motivations for doing them produce anything but life. These must be identified, confronted and rooted out before real health can be restored.

Workaholism

My family suffers from an inherited disease. My minister father has it. My brothers and sisters have it. I have it. It manifests something like this: "If I'm not working to exhaustion, I'm not working hard enough." Fun wastes precious ministry time. Time for fun, therefore, means time for guilt. Exercise cuts into time for work. More guilt. Then guilt for not exercising. Even sleep distracts from the essential task of ministering, working and producing. Forget hobbies. Hobbies are for the uncommitted who have time for such trivial pursuits. The answer to this one should be so obvious I should not have to waste the words to spell it out.

In warring against this tendency, my wife and I found some solutions that worked for us. For example, we bought a week at a timeshare condominium on the north shore of Lake Pend Oreille in north Idaho a couple of hours from where we lived at the time. We really could not afford it, but we knew we needed something like it. For that week each year, we left our children with their grandmother while the two of us spent a week alone together in shameless self-indulgence. And God approved so heartily that He enabled us to pay for it! Find a way to cultivate a healthy measure of "holy selfishness." Indulge!

One afternoon in the depth of burnout when I was too tired to work—but lacked the courage to leave the office and actually *look* like I was not working—God said simply, *Instead of feeling guilty for these stolen moments, why not thank Me for this opportunity to rest?* Obediently, I began a simple but refreshing discipline of doing just that for a few moments each day. Try it! For a while you will feel like a kid with your hand in the forbidden cookie jar, but you will like it just the same and it may help save your sanity.

The old adage says, "All work and no play makes Jack a dull boy." Playtime can be holy time. I used to feel guilty for taking time out when the friend I mentioned earlier would come to my house and jokingly ask my wife if I could come out and play. A good laugh serves at least as well as twenty minutes in prayer for release of tension and refreshment to the soul. "A joyful heart is good medicine, but a broken spirit dries up the bones" (Proverbs 17:22). Take time for things you enjoy, and reject the guilt.

The Necessity of Exercise

On another occasion the Lord spoke to me on the issue of exercise to say, *If you don't start exercising, you're going to die.* Although I knew I stood in no immediate danger of losing my life in the literal sense, I knew there was serious risk of losing something important to my life that could not easily be recovered. On my father's side I belong to the Osage Nation—a once-powerful Native American tribe now located in Oklahoma. We Osage have been culturally conditioned to worship strength, both spiritual and physical. Never in my life had I known serious weakness up until this point. Strength was a gift I took for granted and from which I drew great pride.

Ever since God formed man from the dust of the earth and breathed His personal spirit into him, body and spirit have been interdependent. Physical health profoundly affects spiritual health, and vice versa. The stresses associated with burnout had rendered my body weak and sick, and it was affecting me spiritually and emotionally as well.

I needed to begin an exercise regimen but could not find the energy to do it on my own, despite the Lord's warning. History has taught me, however, that when I fail to obey the Lord freely, He will set up a situation that compels me to do so. Not that He violates my free will! It is just that I gave Him blanket permission long ago to deal with me as He chooses, and I have never withdrawn it. My father (the earthly one) began to notice the deterioration in my health and purchased a membership for me at a local athletic club. Because he had spent the money, my personal obligation pattern clicked in—beneficially for once—and I began to exercise. I chose bodybuilding because I enjoyed growing muscles and experiencing the pumped feeling that follows a good set. For you, it might be racquetball, jogging or swimming. The point is that exercise plays a crucial role in the recovery of any burnout victim.

I kept up the discipline for many years until injuries to my spine ended it. Until then I attacked it with the same intensity I typically invest in anything I do. Before I stopped I had built 28-inch thighs, 18-inch biceps and a 48-inch chest. Because an intimidating physique is hardly an asset to a pastor, I probably would have stopped anyway and chosen some other form of physical fitness. Later, I began riding a bike in the summer and skiing in the winter.

In the beginning I felt guilty for spending so much time on something unrelated to my work, but I soon learned that the gym or the slopes were places where I could escape talking shop and settling everyone's deep life problems. In the gym and on the slopes I could be just another human being, rather than a ministry machine or superman. If I wanted to pray, I could, even while grunting out reps or fearing for my life in midair as I jumped off a high cornice.

As an added benefit, I got to rub elbows with the real world, not just the members of the church locked up in the "Christian ghetto." Every Christian leader needs that kind of contact, not just for leading people to Jesus, but to keep him in touch with real people and real needs.

I am no physician, so feel free to accept or reject what I am about to say, depending on whether I make sense to you. My body knows—and my chiropractor at that time confirmed—that the body produces and stores stress toxins in its tissues when it cannot filter them out quickly enough. Over a period of time these can damage the digestive system, weaken muscles and ligaments and alter body chemistry in ways that affect our moods and mental processes, among other things. Stress can be particularly hard on the heart and the adrenal gland.

Exercise helps eliminate these stored toxins and aids in restoring healthy body chemistry. It strengthens the heart muscle, helps the adrenal gland begin secreting adrenaline normally once more and restores weakened connective tissues, tendons and ligaments. All of this helps reduce and eliminate the physical pain and chronic illness so many burnout victims experience and that their doctors have such a difficult time diagnosing. It also helps reestablish an overall sense of well-being and helps renew the body's ability to withstand emotional stress and physical disease.

I recommend that you see your personal physician for a complete physical exam to determine what level of exercise you can safely undertake and at what degree of intensity. Since you have depleted your nutritional reserves, consider asking him or her to refer you to a qualified nutritionist who can help you rebuild those reserves. At a minimum, you should clean up your diet. Most of us today have at least a basic awareness of what food is healthy and what food is not. So just do it!

After your checkup, go to an athletic club or gym where good instruction can be found. In a community large enough to present options, shop around and ask questions until you find which club has the best instructors. Tell your instructor about the results of your physical exam, explain whatever personal goals you might have for exercising and then let the professional design an enjoyable program appropriate and effective for you. Or simply go shopping for a pair of in-line roller skates or running shoes. The point is to get at it!

For the first month or more, you may feel a bit sick both during and after your workouts. Unaccustomed to exertion, you may experience headaches as a result of your workouts. Each of your early workouts will be a burden and you will be tempted to quit. Some days you will feel as though you are just too tired to go. Ignore all of this. Your body is cleansing itself as your cells release those stored toxins into your bloodstream where your natural filters can eliminate them. Expect to feel a bit "off" for a while. Stay with it faithfully and you will find yourself a confirmed "sweat hog," addicted to the satisfying, full sensation of pumped-up and fatigued muscles. You will look better and you will feel better in every way. More than this, you will find your energy returning.

Do not con yourself into thinking you are too far gone or too tired to do this. Exercise is too important to your recovery for you to permit this kind of self-deception. There will be no full and permanent recovery without physical exercise of some kind. God intended us to cultivate a healthy balance between body and spirit.

Breaking the Isolation Pattern

For church leaders, what I have to say concerning this pattern may threaten some cherished theologies concerning church life and government, and I make no apology for it. Most of this section is specifically aimed at pastors, but much of it applies just as well to lay leaders and even to those in management positions in the world.

By design, most patterns of government practiced in the modern church keep the pastor isolated and deprive him of any real power to lead. No one ever consciously intended that result, but the effect often remains. Too many churches today continue to practice a democratic form of government in which the task of those in positions of leadership is to carry out the will of the people as expressed in the vote of the majority or through a popularly elected board.

This works well in secular government, but not in God's house. God never intended His church to be a democracy carrying out the will of the people. He formed His church as a theocracy, ruled by Him through His anointed and appointed servants who discern and carry out His will—and who have both freedom and authority to do so. Moses did not rise to leadership through an electoral process, nor did Peter or Paul. God Himself appointed them and gave them authority to set direction. Each of them maintained a team for balance and for counsel, but above all their teams were *their* teams, not groups of people thrust upon them by some democratic process of selection.

Because so many churches function as democracies rather than as theocracies, elders (or their equivalents) whom God intended to function as the pastor's team in ministry are elected by the people rather than appointed by authority as the Scriptures dictate. In case after case, therefore, they fail to function as the pastor's team. In fact, they often attain their positions because factions opposed to the pastor placed them in office to insure dissenting voices in high places. My father pastored a series of Congregational churches as I grew up, and I watched this dynamic develop again and again. The results can be devastating, both to the church and to the pastor as unbiblical structures of authority cripple his ability to carry out the vision God has given him.

Because we operate our churches on nonbiblical bases, we burn out our shepherds. The pastor too often stands alone, rather than in the midst of a trusted team with whom he genuinely shares his vision and ministry. I often hear ministers speaking of this isolation and seeking ways to break out of it. The suggested solution is usually to seek fellowship among fellow clergy, but I find this terribly inadequate. This kind of sharing and uplift requires more time than most of us have available. Further, I know that for my own primary support system to be effective, the participants must be with me in the daily crush of ministry. Although I need fellowship with other clergy to keep a certain perspective, I have a greater need for people to stand alongside me who live and labor in my own situation, who carry the same burden and who understand the unique pressures of our own church.

I rarely feel the isolation anymore in the way that I did in the days when the first church I planted functioned under a form of democracy rather than theocracy. In those days, no matter what crisis we faced I found myself standing alone. The elected board seemed paralyzed and unable to learn to minister effectively with me, having little or no ability to stand firm under fire for the sake of the flock. Everyone suffered for it.

Today I have both full-time and part-time staff whom I regard as elders. They constitute my primary team. Together we lead the church in spiritual matters, as God has called us to do. Our administrative board works with me and with our staff on matters financial and contractual, but my staff team leads in all other areas as they have been called and anointed to do. We share the burden, cultivate vulnerability and face crises together. For me, professional isolation has largely become a thing of the past.

Clearly, unbiblical forms of church government constitute a major cause of burnout among ministry professionals. If the specific system under which you labor fails to align with God's Word, I would have a difficult time telling you how to change it. The uniqueness of every situation—and the Bible itself—leaves much latitude for the form a valid theocratic government might take. I can only say that under any system, the pastor or anointed lay leader must seek out those called to be close to and safe for him. Would the same not be true for a leader in business or the corporate world? Gather a team of trustworthy people and utilize their gifts, both in ministry to the flock and for your own support. Ask God to reveal these people to you and then intentionally draw them to yourself. If you feel too far gone to do this effectively, then ask God Himself to sovereignly bring them into your life.

Some of you have been so badly burned and betrayed by trusted confidants and team members that relationship like this may seem too difficult—too much risk. It seemed this way to me at one time because I, too, had been deeply scarred by people I loved and trusted. In truth, I had chosen the wrong people and had yet to learn how to identify the faithful and true. But even through the bad choices I learned wisdom. That being said, I never forget that even Jesus chose a Judas.

Breaking the Self-abuse Pattern

The self-abuse pattern often grows from a subconscious death wish. Life feels like a burden and you would really just like to die, and so you poison yourself with practices certain to further destroy your already deteriorating body. While the process may be subconscious, you may have enough awareness to recognize the morbid pleasure you take in it. In either case it must be stopped.

Common manifestations include destructive patterns of diet and rest. Your eating habits have probably been atrocious, marked by irregular meal times and junk food eaten on the run. When given the opportunity for a really good meal, you eat too hurriedly. You overeat. You under eat. Certain food allergies or addictions may appear. As I indicated earlier, you should consult a qualified nutritionist and begin to rebuild depleted reserves. Determine to eat regularly. Decide to eat whole grains and other natural, unprocessed foods. No mystery here! Just good sense. And while you do it, remember that your life depends on it as well as the glory of God in you.

Most pastors and key leaders in any walk of life regularly violate the Sabbath. God designed us to function best when we take one day in seven to stop, worship God and do restful things that we enjoy. We pay a high price for violating this natural law, not so much as an expression of the wrath of God as in reaping the consequences of arguing with reality. Are you a pastor? Do not expect to accomplish a Sabbath rest on Sunday since Sunday constitutes the biggest workday of the week. Choose another day and then leave the phone off the hook. Not a bad plan for business owners and managers as well!

Most of us wounded ones suffer from workaholism that compels us to work average weeks of sixty hours at a minimum. And we love it so! What noble martyrs we are! For the layperson fully dedicated to ministry, this often translates into forty hours or more at a secular job and then twenty or more for the church, all of which takes a toll on the body and the spirit. Unless I guard against it, even today I find myself racing from one set of demands to another at breakneck speed, leaving no room for rest between tasks, much less the kind of meditation in prayer that renews the soul and energizes life. I used to tell myself that I perform best when under that kind of pressure. It can be fun, but it cannot last.

In reality, you are the car that rounds a corner at a hundred miles per hour, only to plow into the wall the driver failed to see coming. Almost without warning life comes crashing to a stop and you find yourself emotionally, intellectually, creatively and physically destroyed. Recovery can be exceedingly difficult. Most of us with this personality type may never learn to actually see the wall coming, but we must at least learn to know where and when it will most likely appear and then slow down before impact. This requires the establishment of more reasonable patterns of rest and relaxation, even before any sense of fatigue sets in. One inch from the wall can feel the same as ten miles.

Try delegating the management of your schedule to someone you trust. My secretary, for instance, does a much better job than I do of telling people that I have no spots open for three weeks. I feel obligated to make room for them, no matter what the cost to myself. She does not. Let trusted others create windows of rest in your busy schedule. In the long run, this can spell the difference between sanity and breakdown.

Breaking the Old Prayer Patterns

Your prayer life has probably failed to refresh you for quite some time, if it has not evaporated altogether. On close inspection you will likely find that it needed revamping anyway. Most of us have been fed a diet of pietistic legalism that tells us we must invest at least a half hour alone with God every day. Do not misunderstand. My goal remains to spend at least that much daily time with my Lord, but times of burnout signal a need for change.

Perhaps you have been taught a particular method of prayer and devotion. Certain styles of language must be used. You begin with "Dear God," as if you were writing a letter, and you end with "in Jesus' name," in the same way you would sign a letter "Sincerely yours." I learned from my parents to listen to God during my daily devotional, to be silent before Him to hear His voice or to receive Scripture references to look up. I still do this, and I write in a notebook what I hear.

But during burnout all of this became an empty ritual. I felt lost without my notebook, as if I could not pray without all the elements of the ritual present. Under normal circumstances method helps, but the deeply burned-out servant of God often needs radical change. At first, as my prayer discipline began to falter, I felt guilty for spending so little time "on my knees" and so I would strive with all my fading strength to put it back together again. When I inevitably failed, I fell into deeper guilt. At last I heard the Lord order me to stop.

The old pattern, steeped in method and legalism, had lost its effectiveness. God wanted to do larger things through me, and for that I needed a renewed means of communing with Him.

God loves to do things "out of the box." In the midst of my devotional dysfunction I heard God say, *I'll not speak to you as to other men.*

"How then?" I pled in confusion.

Trust your instincts, came the reply.

As I pondered what that might mean, I realized that He intended to rebuild my shattered confidence and teach me to trust in what He had been so carefully building into me through brokenness. In the process it suddenly struck me that nowhere does the Bible mandate anything concerning forms of daily devotions other than to pray without ceasing (see 1 Thessalonians 5:17) and to take in some piece of God's Word daily for the heart to continually meditate on (see Psalm 119 and others). Good news! This leaves plenty of room for creativity and change.

The Lord began to train into me a new awareness of how to pray without ceasing and how to meditate on His Word. Rather than block out time in which to expend energy and force a level of concentration I could no longer generate, I could simply plant some portion of the Word in my mind and heart and let it resonate there all day long. I found that I subconsciously meditated on whatever I put into my heart. Insights would later float up out of nowhere, as if the computer had been running a background program and finally produced the solution. My very instincts could be infused with the Word, and I could be more responsive to the need of the moment than I had been previously. Best of all, it required less conscious effort.

In healthier times, one of my desires had been to steep the entire day more deeply in prayer, rather than relegate it exclusively to my daily devotional hour. In this time of expanded freedom, I began to pray more in tongues than in

English. The energy expenditure diminished while the return in power increased. As I made the changes, even though some of them were only temporary, I found myself more alive to the prompting of the Spirit in the moment.

Ironically, my traditional daily devotional hour had actually begun to get in the way of real communication with God. Patterns of rote habit had taken over where the give and take of real relationship should have been. Since then I have come to know God's presence in a new way. I later returned to a disciplined practice of daily meditative prayer, but it had new life and flexibility in it.

So, let God both destroy and rebuild your pattern for prayer and Scripture study, and refuse to allow yourself to feel guilty if it seems as though you have not been praying or studying at all for a time. Shut out those religious voices that tell you God will do nothing if you fail to pray. God is not that small. If He had to be limited to responding to the puny actions I am able to take as a finite human being, my faith would be a sorry one indeed. Besides, your guilt will vanish when the newer, more adequate form emerges. Allow for experimentation and failure in the meantime.

Begin breaking patterns by confessing your helplessness, and then call upon the Lord to rescue you. It is a time-honored cry, proven to bear fruit.

7

LIVING WITH A THIRD STAGE
BURNOUT VICTIM

In my situation, my wife escaped most of what I suffered and was able to support me in my recovery. Her invincibly positive nature formed a good counterbalance to my once melancholy one, and I write this chapter from the wellspring of her instinctive wisdom in dealing with me. I realize, however, that in some cases husband and wife together suffer third stage incapacities. For their sakes I have done my best to address the unique problems that result when neither husband nor wife can provide one another the support they so desperately need.

If you find that both of you are wounded at the same time, you will be strongly tempted to see one another as the enemy. In your dysfunction, mutual need becomes mutual demand, which sets you up to fail. Disappointed demand becomes anger. Poorly processed anger turns lovers into enemies. Because neither of you deals adequately with even normal household pressures, very small irritations quickly grow into very large ones. Chances are that you have never been real partners in sharing emotions anyway, even in your healthy days. This does not always hold true, but it happens often enough to make mention of it here. The present situation, therefore, may widen a hidden crack into a gaping chasm.

No matter how incapacitated you feel, the first mental discipline you must strive to exercise is to identify the real enemy and resolve not to attack your mate. Your enemy is the situation you face—not your partner. If you cannot yet face things together and learn to talk out your feelings with one another, then at least learn not to attack. Even if I could give you a multistep plan for accomplishing this, you would be unable to follow it. I can only say directly and simply that by God's grace you must make the effort. If necessary, get a trusted third party to help you, but get it done. I myself have spent a number of hours interpreting wounded spouses to wounded spouses. It helps.

Prepare for Loneliness

The burnout victim desperately needs his "space." "Down" time, spent alone, is crucial to his recovery, so if your spouse is wounded and you remain functional, be prepared to carry more than your share of the weight in the household. He no longer has the capacity to deal effectively or consistently with daily stresses and responsibilities. It may seem to you that he will never rebound from his pain, but he will, unless you compound it with misunderstanding and misplaced pressures.

It will be a lonely time for you—a time for surrendering your own life and your own needs, while one who may once have been strong limps through a period of weakness. Listen sympathetically to his hurts, fears, depressions and angers, but refuse to wallow in them together. At all costs remain positive. He does not need the pressure you create by becoming angry with him or by insensitively demanding that he do things to correct his condition or his behavior.

Believe in Him and for Him

Above all, believe in him when he can no longer believe in himself. My wife used to position herself directly in my face—the only time I could tolerate the pressure of direct frontal communication—and firmly tell me I was a good pastor, a good father and a good man. I needed to hear it. I knew too well that my performance at home had deteriorated, and her words encouraged me to hold on to my identity.

Your wounded one may have lost all faith that God will choose to conquer the situation. In this case, you must maintain faith on his behalf, no matter how difficult it may seem. The wounded one hangs by a thread, a decision of his will— "white-knuckling it," if he's hanging on at all, neither feeling nearness to God nor even believing in God's willingness to help. If you can believe for him without preaching sermons, you help rebuild his faith.

If both of you are wounded, then, as a couple, find someone outside the marriage to do for you what one of you can no longer do for the other in this area. It may be a time of distance in your relationship, which renders you extraordinarily vulnerable. Because of this vulnerability, under no circumstances should you seek help or support from a member of the opposite sex individually, outside the marriage. I scarcely need to spell out the dangers that lie down that path. Seek out that person or persons together and get help jointly. It would be good to find another couple. Better yet if you have a small group that meets regularly for prayer, ministry and fellowship. Share deeply in that setting. Let them believe in you and reaffirm your callings as individuals and as a couple.

Preserve an Orderly Environment

If you are the whole one and your mate is wounded, do all you can to keep the household running smoothly. Maintain a light atmosphere, happy and orderly. The comfort and refuge of home are a healing balm to the burnout victim. At this point in his life home can too easily become a place of pressure that drives him outside to find "space" and peace. Remember that cognitive distortions can make things seem different than they are and that through the filter of pain problems can be easily magnified out of proportion to reality. Outside the home, his vulnerability can open him to those who would prey upon his emotional need. Home must be a place where he knows he will not be wounded further.

Gracefully Leave Him There

If you find your burnout victim sitting alone in a stupor somewhere, eyes glazed, staring into space, gracefully leave him there and deal with the household on your own. He will be fine and will come out of it eventually. Your demands will only drive him further into withdrawal and could even spark an angry outburst. Countless times Beth found me sitting at the kitchen table, staring into a plate of food or contemplating the grain of the wood in the tabletop, lost to the world. A simple hug around the shoulders with no accompanying demand for response poured medicine into my ailing spirit. She would then go on about her business, praying for me all the while, and I felt it.

Exercise Self-control

If both of you are wounded, you must exercise as much self-control as you can muster. Again, I say that you must strive not to identify one another as the enemy. It may help to learn to recognize when household pressures have been building on the two of you and resolve to go out together for a while before one or both of you explode. Get a sitter for the kids and see a movie or take a walk. Anything to break the pattern and get out of the pressured environment!

In every case in which I have seen two burnout victims at war with one another in a marriage relationship, deep-seated problems of another kind clearly fed into it. Those problems existed long before the wounding from outside the marriage began, and they only surfaced in force when the couple's normal restraining strengths wore thin. Remember that the pressure of burnout opens hidden cracks and exposes concealed weaknesses so that changes can be made.

By contrast, couples who are whole as individuals seem to survive well even when both parties are wounded. I believe that when mortal combat in the home accompanies burnout produced by outside forces, the ultimate source is often a wise and loving God who deliberately aggravates our brokenness so that we will take note, face the hidden issues and resolve them.

I have seen wounded couples in burnout face their inner issues and not only survive but come through it more whole and clean than before the onset of suffering forced the issue. God healed old wounds and sins and enabled them to recover together.

Prayer Cover

If you are the whole one, cover your sufferer with a blanket of prayer every waking hour. It will give you a sense of being helpful, rather than standing by helplessly, and real power will be released to mend your partner's wounds. As I have counseled already, do not encourage him in ways that demand performance, and refrain from telling him the content of your prayers for him. He will feel obligated for your sake to try to make it all happen, and that only deepens the condition.

When both of you are wounded, find someone outside of your marriage to pray this way for you, because neither of you will be able to do it consistently for the other. Make certain this person understands your condition, and then trust him or her.

Stand Guard

Out in the world, the healthy one in the relationship must keep a sharp lookout for those who may be hanging around the wounded one. If your wounded one holds a leadership position in the church, people tend to press in on him, demanding ministry with no concept of, or care for, his personal condition.

Begin by guarding his heart with prayer. With the help of Father God, be strong in your own spirit and, in an almost mystical way, carry the bleeding heart of your burnout victim in your own bosom. Lift his pain to the Father on his behalf. "Bear one another's burdens, and thereby fulfill the law of Christ" (Galatians 6:2).

Intervene physically when appropriate. For instance, at church my wife sometimes noticed that a certain person known for being a "leech" had me cornered and was droning on and on while I turned ghastly shades of gray. She would come quickly to my side to strengthen me silently in prayer, forming a shield in the spirit. And I would be further strengthened simply by not being alone.

Beth also had a special sensitivity concerning those who would take advantage of my vulnerability, that Distant Early Warning System I wrote about earlier. She warned me many times and I learned to heed her. She left me free to listen or not, and did not add to the pressure by insisting that I actually act on her warnings. She merely stated the facts and then left me alone to consider them.

Often she headed people off by getting to them herself before they could get to me. She did it so nicely and subtly that the potential troublemaker seldom had any awareness of what had just happened. For all anyone else knew, she was just the usual friendly happy Beth coming to visit.

Never do this sort of thing in an obvious way that lets the one you want to head off know that you are angry or being protective. You will only look bad in their eyes and create new tensions with others, which your wounded one will have to deal with later.

When both of you are wounded and in need of protection, I again advise you to alert trusted others to do for you what you may be unable to do for one another. You will find, however, that even in the depth of wounding, your personal protective instincts remain active and functional. To a certain degree, you can continue to exercise protective functions for one another, no matter what your condition. I think this is so because you perceive a threat to your mate as a threat to yourself. In your wounding, your paranoia keeps those protective instincts alive.

Up to a point these instincts are reliable. The problem for the burnout victim, however, is one of balance and a tendency to carry a special sensitivity for trouble beyond the bounds of reality. Cognitive distortions quickly become full-blown delusions if not watched carefully. Seek, therefore, to be disciplined enough not to turn the protective words you speak to your mate into demands that must be responded to. Then use the checks and balances provided by those trusted others I spoke of to control your own tendency to lose perspective.

If you are the functional one in the relationship, be acutely aware at all times that those who wounded your partner were probably trusted friends, people with whom he risked himself, people into whom he poured his time, love and energy. They have stabbed him in the back and cut his heart to ribbons. The problem may not be one of forgiveness. He may already have accomplished that. It is just that emotional woundings are much like physical ones. They take time to heal, even after medicine has been applied and the irritant removed. The process will probably take much longer to complete than you think you can bear, but it does run its course. Learn patience in the meantime and do not betray his confidence. Share with no one what he shares with you.

> "Let everyone be on guard against his neighbor, and do not trust any brother; because every brother deals craftily, and every neighbor goes about as a slanderer. Everyone deceives his neighbor and does not speak the truth, they have taught their tongue to speak lies; they weary themselves committing iniquity. Your dwelling is in the midst of deceit; through deceit they refuse to know Me," declares the LORD.
>
> Jeremiah 9:4–6

> Even my close friend in whom I trusted, who ate my bread, has lifted up his heel against me.
>
> Psalm 41:9

Cover for Him

Deep wounds from betrayals such as these often take years to heal. As you conceal from others what your wounded one has shared with you, conceal his general condition as well. In every way help him preserve a public image of strong functionality. No one, except those the burnout victim approves, needs to know how he really feels. If asked, say, "He's all right, but you can pray for us; it never hurts." Do not risk giving anyone ammunition that might be used later to add to the problem of wounding and burnout. Do not risk damaging your partner's trust in you. He may have no place else to go, and his trust in you can spell the difference between survival and complete breakdown.

While you preserve a functional public image, take care not to undermine your partner's self-esteem by taking up too much of the slack he leaves, either at home, at work or in the ministry. Better to lend just a little help in the performance of a task than to do it all for him. Better even to let some tasks go undone than to add to his guilt burden by doing jobs he knows and accepts as his own.

Set Personal Needs Aside

Your own needs will have to be set aside for a while. The one in deep wounding cannot meet them. He will try, but he really has nothing to work with. Your response to his incapacity can be either healing or immeasurably destructive. I know of one wife who—wounded by her husband's incapacity to meet her needs, and not understanding the reason for it—turned to the attack and accused him of everything from lack of love to hypocrisy in his faith and ministry. She pushed and pushed until he exploded. His raw nerves could not take the pressure.

To show love, to pay attention to a new dress or to appreciate how well a household task was accomplished is often beyond his capability. He has nothing left to give and no amount of spiritual or emotional grunting on his part will produce it. The burnout victim knows his failure. In fact, the guilt of it is driving him deeper into burnout, but he can do almost nothing to change it.

You will have to learn to draw from the Lord alone what you need to sustain your own emotional health. If you have children in the home, you must find the faith to believe that God knew what shape their wounded parent would be in and that He has already provided for their survival, turning all things to good (see Romans 8:28). Sometimes I was so "gone" that the very presence of my wonderful children made me want to scream in desperation. Try as I might, I could not respond to them as they needed me to, no matter how much I longed to. Their little voices seemed like daggers carving chunks off my already bleeding nerves.

Family members often had to repeat things to me two and three times to make their messages understood. I could hear the sound they made, but my mind could make no sense of what I heard. I would ask for things to be repeated again and again until the kids gave up and got their mother to tell me. I can still hear her carefully instructing, "Get in his face. Make certain you have eye contact. Ask him if he is listening. Then ask him to repeat what you said. If that doesn't work, come get me."

Beth had wisdom enough not to criticize me for my inability. She knew what kind of man I am under normal circumstances and therefore granted me room to recover. I gave to the children as I could, and I knew Beth covered for me when I could not. On the whole, however, she tells me I did well with the children. I knew that as children they could never understand what was happening to their father and so I made extra effort.

Worried about your children? My son is 33 years old at this writing. From childhood he has been a burden bearer, incredibly prophetically sensitive to others' feelings. As a child of only eight and nine years, therefore, he sensed my exhaustion and decided in his own heart to make no demands of me, not to burden me with his own developing needs. He therefore closed himself off from me emotionally and began to face his life crises without my help. Later, this vow not to burden me became a bitterness and a barrier between us that we have successfully worked through over the years together. God is good. Burnout takes its toll on everyone associated with the burnout victim, but for every hurt, our Lord provides a means to heal.

Through it all Beth learned more deeply than ever how to derive her sense of self-worth and beauty from the Lord. She learned to sense when He noticed and when He complimented her at the times when I could not. She "embraced her fireball" in the form of her own loneliness and allowed it to work purification in her heart as it drove her directly to her Lord. As a result, she outgrew the need for me to supply what I could no longer supply. Then, when I began to recover, nurturing and affirming her again, she was delighted, but not dependent.

Standing Together

Most of what I have written here comes from the perspective of a man supported by his wife. I need to emphasize that when wives are wounded and husbands retain functionality, the task remains the same. Husbands and wives share partnership in ministry and in life, and the partnership must be defended. Do not think that Beth's and my relationship is more important than our ministry, but rather that we share ministry as a centerpiece of our union. We minister together as one flesh. In fact, our ministry is a major part of why our marriage works so well. Like warriors who fight back to back, we guard one another from attack even as we advance and take ground from the adversary. When one goes down, the other stands guard so that the partnership is preserved. Neither of us works as well alone as we do together.

In 1984 Beth and I were scheduled to teach and lead worship at a national gathering of the renewal movement in the denomination we were then part of. Just a few days before our scheduled departure, however, Beth was admitted to the hospital with acute abdominal pain. A day later, surgeons removed a cyst the size of a grapefruit from her left fallopian tube. After the surgery she nearly died from an allergic reaction to morphine.

I could have gone to the meeting and Beth would have been fine in the hospital, but the Holy Spirit clearly told me not to go. I needed to stay home and guard my wounded partner for the sake of our love and our ministry together. For three days, therefore, I spent every spare moment in the hospital, by her bedside holding her hand.

Distressing numbers of ministers' wives suffer at home because of the energy they invest for little thanks and because of the tongues that wag in criticism. In many fellowships the minister's spouse does as much work as he does, and in nearly every aspect of the ministry. She, too, can burn out in the service of the Lord and needs the same care her husband would require if he were wounded. Unfortunately, too many husbands/pastors lack a full sense of partnership and so neglect the wounded one on the home front. They often continue to pursue their ministries, all but blind to the plight of their mates. Some of my current staff are licensed and ordained women. I pray first that they do not burn out under my leadership, and second that their husbands support them as my wife has supported me.

Do Not Take Responsibility

Finally, in no way take personal responsibility for your wounded mate's recovery. What he suffers is an issue to be settled ultimately between him and his Lord. You can pray, support, love and listen. You can avoid being part of the problem and you can help by creating an environment conducive to healing, but in the end you may not turn out to be a key part of the solution. The solution can only be found between him and his Father God. They must settle the issues between themselves and you can do little to help. Grant him the room to hash it out within himself without joining him in his bitterness, preaching at him or offering unsolicited counsel. The result in your recovered partner will be increased wisdom, balance, stability, power and all the fruits of the Spirit. It is worth waiting for.

8

LINGERING QUESTIONS

How Long Will My Recovery Take?

Speed of recovery depends on a number of factors. How healthy were you before you sank into burnout? How strong is your general makeup, both physically and emotionally? What kind of support systems are available to you to aid and assist in your healing? What kinds of pressures continue to drain your energy? Is good counsel available? Under any circumstances, recovery is usually a lengthy sojourn. It takes months or even years for the deeply burned out to return fully to strength, so prepare yourself emotionally for an extended process. You have expended resources that cannot easily be replaced and you must give yourself time to rebuild them.

Will I Recover Completely?

Yes and no. You may never fully recover the level of intensity, strength and resilience you enjoyed before you burned out. Unfortunately, you have squandered an only partially renewable resource and you will henceforth and forever be compelled to measure your limited strength against the size of the tasks that come your way. You will have gained wisdom more valuable and more life giving than the resources you lost. You may, therefore, actually become more productive with less expenditure of energy than you thought possible. You will discover that you are much less easily thrown off balance emotionally. Your sense of perspective will be razor sharp.

What about Relapses?

You will probably experience many relapses in the course of your recovery. For a long time, if I overextended myself for too long a period, I would suddenly feel completely undone, as if there had been no recovery at all. Such episodes mean little. Rest and a stronger sense of perspective provide the cure.

For a while you may feel like a bouncing ball, sometimes descending to the depths of your former despair, sometimes bouncing out and flying high. Or you may descend to stage one and then recover quickly, only to plunge to the very bottom a week later. Having done so, you may awaken the next morning wondering what the whole thing was about, after all, because you feel so wonderful once more. Remember that recovery takes time and that temporary relapses are part of the process.

What If My Mate Will Not Stop Putting Pressure on Me to Perform When I Can't?

This is not an uncommon problem, especially for female victims! Too many husbands fail to understand the condition, thinking it is all nonsense and denying that it even exists. Because of this they continue making selfish physical and emotional demands of her, condemning her if she cannot produce, and ultimately placing her in danger of serious

112

breakdown. This can happen to men, as well, but the victims of this kind of misunderstanding are most often women.

Much of my answer to this question was included in chapter 7, but I will add one more dimension here. As a last resort, when a mate refuses to come to terms with your needs, a temporary separation may be in order until you have had time to regain your strength and balance. The pain of your absence may serve to bring about needed humility and understanding in your mate, and you will find the space you desperately need to begin rebuilding your lost strength.

Set aside any nice religious legalisms you may have accumulated concerning God's command that married people should stay together no matter what. If you have fallen deeply into incapacity and your mate refuses to understand and grant you the grace you need, then you must separate temporarily for the two of you to remain together. In fact, if you fail to get some distance, the alternative may be forced separation in the form of extended hospitalization.

Wives in burnout must often therefore forget (temporarily) all those misapplied scriptures about wifely submission. Healing has little to do with issues of submission, but rather with recovering enough strength to enable you once again to actively submit in a healthy partnership (see Ephesians 5:21–24).

Why Did God Let This Happen to Me?

Read on.

PART II

THE DARK NIGHT OF THE SOUL

I am a warrior
I have fought long
Until sweat stings my eyes
And tears choke my battle cry
Fight on!

When youth's exuberance and morning's hope
bleed red upon the ground
Then wisdom's steady hand keeps on.

Sweat-burned eyes do see
While tear-choked throat soars free in song.

What must be done
What must be sung
I win because I cannot lose.
I live for I have learned to die.

Loren Sandford, March 1996

9

THE DARK NIGHT
OF THE SOUL

After my season of burnout God granted me a couple of good years of recovered health and strength before a new chapter began, one deeper and more painful than I could have dreamed of. It began with a series of devastating disasters compressed into a period of less than a year.

A beloved foster family in our church had adopted thirteen "unadoptable" children, in addition to their own four by birth. While on a cross-country trip as a family one of the children suffered a fatal accident. Virginia authorities arrested them and charged them with murder. Conviction and imprisonment followed. I suffered through both trials, fuming and frustrated at the media circus going on around me and at the miscarriage of justice both trials represented.

One of my trusted staff members committed adultery with three women in the church and had to be dismissed. Because I could not reveal the whole story for the sake of the women who had been victimized, I stood accused of being too harsh. People left the church over it.

We built a new church building with a loan from our denomination, fell behind in payments and then were forced to withdraw from the denomination because of apostate actions taken by General Synod. I had to fire a youth pastor for serious errors in judgment. Again, people left the church who failed to understand the serious nature of the cause.

A fallen pastor who had been with us for a process of healing and restoration left to plant a church six miles away and took a block of people with him in spite of my reservations. Each of these crises cost us in uncounted ways and affected us more deeply—and me more personally—than I can begin to say here.

All of these crises and a host of lesser ones blew the heart out of our church. We began losing members. Elders left, burned out and exhausted over the long years of struggle, and angry with me in ways and for issues that made no sense to me at the time.

The IRS audited my personal tax returns, and because of the incompetence of my tax accountant and my own sinful willingness to remain ignorant of what he was doing, I was assessed $8,500 in back taxes and interest at a time when an assessment like that could have sent my family into bankruptcy. The news of the results came while I was away on an extended ministry trip, so my wife had to absorb the blow at home alone. Then both of my girls were threatened sexually while I was away on the same ministry trip and unable to be home to be their strength.

During the same period of time, after months of struggle, I finally decided to leave my home of twelve years where my entire family lived (father, mother and siblings), resign from the church I had planted and pastored for most of that time and move to Denver to become the executive pastor of a megachurch. Contrary to what had been presented during the negotiation stage, the system there was in trouble. I appeared as the "stepfather" to replace the senior pastor who wanted to be free to pursue his music career without really letting go of the church.

People were angry at his absence and disturbed by a host of other issues. I represented a poor attempt to mollify them. I could not blame them for not buying it. For many of the same reasons, staff had trouble accepting my entry into the system as well. Finally, I found my most precious values either thrust aside or, in some cases, ridiculed by my senior pastor. Even had he been able to release what needed to be released, it was simply a bad fit. I did not belong, and by the time I resigned fourteen months later, every good gift I had ever been confident of had been maligned, from my preaching and teaching to my music.

After leaving that church, I endured three hellish months—unemployed and under a hail of gunfire—carefully discerning the Lord's will for my future, afraid that I had led my career and my family into a terrible dead end. The move had been hard on them, and I felt their pain acutely. All of these crises were only the beginning of a season of crushing more deep and furious than I could have imagined during the burnout years.

In the end, a series of miracles and signs confirmed the Lord's guidance to plant a new church in the north end of the Denver metro area where a whole new set of pressures and betrayals awaited me.

Falling into the Abyss

At times, burnout feels as if you are hanging on to the edge of a cliff by your fingernails, afraid that you will fall and that God will not be there to catch you. In the wilderness, or the dark night of the soul, you plead, "God, if I suffer anymore, I'll break," and He says, *Right!* End of discussion. Your fingernails snap and you do fall off the cliff, only to find out it is bottomless and that God really will not catch you. Although at some level you know that cannot be true, you feel that way, and no one can convince you otherwise.

In the dark night of the soul there seems to be no sense of the presence, the voice or the blessing of God. You face repeated disasters with little or no perception of His protection. Nothing works. You fail in all you try.

The dark night actually began for me long before the move to Denver. For quite some time it seemed God had been sending me to do things, for which He confirmed the directions miraculously, and then failed to meet me there, withholding the provision I needed to accomplish whatever task He had sent me to do and leaving me alone to struggle with it.

For instance, we built a magnificent building in north Idaho through a series of miracles. We qualified for a loan sufficient only to build a functional shell with no furnishings, but God actually gave us a completely finished and furnished facility with a lighted parking lot. The loan itself was a one-in-ten shot, but it came through. I expected the miracles to continue. God had ordered it and confirmed it; God would pay for it, but within a few months we were $25,000 behind in mortgage payments.

Based on current income and clear needs, I hired staff, only to see the supporting income dry up. I cut expenses to relieve budget deficits, only to see giving drop off in direct proportion to the cuts. I felt abandoned, even betrayed both by people and by God, not to mention confused. Then followed all the other disasters I have spoken of. In the midst of it, my health took a serious turn for the worse. Nothing in my life was left untouched.

I never saw quitting as a live option. I am who I am and I do what I do. I had burned my bridges to other kinds of labor and lifestyle too long ago to reevaluate at this point. A covenant made under God must never be renegotiated. With or without the sense of His presence, and whether or not He seemed to prosper my life and work, I would therefore serve Him.

In the late seventeenth and early eighteenth centuries, Madame Jeanne Guyon, living in France, persecuted and imprisoned by the church, wrote of her own experience of the dark night of the soul. She spoke of a time when the Lord withdraws joy and allows the believer to undergo seasons of persecution even from fellow Christians and those in authority. She wrote of deep seasons of suffering compounded by betrayals on the part of those she trusted most. Her experience of the dark night of the soul included difficulties with health and numerous other forms of loss, including a profound sense of abandonment by the Lord.

Madame Guyon warned of the danger of forsaking the Lord under the emotional pressure of these losses and its accompanying sense of impending spiritual death. "But the true land of promise always lies beyond a vast wasteland. Promise is found only on the far side of a desert," she wrote. And she continued:

> When you can go beyond that place and not seeing your Lord, believe He is there by the eyes of faith alone; When you can walk further and further into Christ when there are no senses, no feelings, not even the slightest registration of the presence of God; when you can sit before Him when everything around you and within you seems to be either falling apart or dead; and when you can come before your Lord without question and without demand, serene in faith alone, and there, before Him, worship Him without distraction, without a great deal of consciousness of self and with no spiritual sense of Him, then will the test of commitment begin to be established. Then will begin the true journey of the Christian life.[1]

I have a passion for testing everything by the Word of God. Just to see that someone somewhere in the history of the church experienced and then explained a thing has never been enough for me. Although I might have that same experience, I need a grounding in God's Word to make sense of it. I have

1. *Final Steps in Christian Maturity* (Jacksonville, Fla.: Christian Books Publishing House, 1985), 35–36.

committed myself to consider, "Is such an experience to be found in the Scripture?" In this case, the answer is unequivocally, yes, such an experience does occur in Scripture. Aside from Job's trials, which we will examine in a later chapter, Psalm 88 perfectly describes the dark night of the soul. As the only psalm in the Bible without a shred of clear hope, it vividly communicates the unvarnished desperation and despair of the author, together with the single most important component for successfully navigating such a time of desolation.

Verses 1–3: "O LORD, the God of my salvation, I have cried out by day and in the night before You. Let my prayer come before You; incline Your ear to my cry! For my soul has had enough troubles, and my life has drawn near to Sheol." Suffering had lasted so long, and affected him so deeply, the psalmist could absorb no more. He felt as if he were about to die, and he deeply longed to do so.

Verse 4: "I am reckoned among those who go down to the pit; I have become like a man without strength." People believed him to be under a divine curse. They saw him as a man on his way to hell who must have been doing something wrong to be suffering like this. The stress of his suffering and the opinions of others broke his strength physically, emotionally and spiritually.

Verse 5: "Forsaken among the dead, like the slain who lie in the grave, whom You remember no more, and they are cut off from Your hand." Believing that God had forgotten him, he had lost his sense of the Lord's nearness. Cut off from his sense of the Lord's life-giving presence, he felt as if he had already died, though his heart still beat.

Verse 6: "You have put me in the lowest pit, in dark places, in the depths." The psalmist knew beyond a doubt that the hand of God had put him in this place of pain. During this period in my own life, I served on the faculty of a three-week-long counseling school in Maryland. During a question-and-answer session, a question arose concerning the nature of the dark night of the soul. I stated that I knew the hand of God was against me and that nothing I did would prosper until He chose to release it. My answer raised quite a controversy, but the psalmist clearly believed that God Himself put him in that place.

Verse 7: "Your wrath has rested upon me, and You have afflicted me with all Your waves." Beyond doubt he believed that some hidden trespass had ignited the Lord's anger with him. Why else would he suffer so? Picture a man struggling to stay upright in a relentless high surf, exhausted by the pounding of the waves. Each time he nearly succeeds in gaining his footing, another wall of water sweeps him off his feet and rolls him over in the sand and grit of the beach, filling his mouth and nostrils with salt. Coughing and retching, he rises, only to be driven under, time and time again. Disaster after disaster. Hurt upon hurt.

Verse 8: "You have removed my acquaintances far from me; You have made me an object of loathing to them; I am shut up and cannot go out." Friends could no longer bear to be around him. His condition frightened and even repulsed them. In the intensity and the duration of his suffering, he stood profoundly alone with no one to truly understand his condition. So overcome was he with grief, trouble and fatigue that he could no longer even bring himself to venture out on the streets. Having experienced the same thing, I know what he meant. Some days I could only stay home, locked up in my home office, unable to face the world with my trembling hands and fragile emotions.

Verse 9: "My eye has wasted away because of affliction; I have called upon You every day, O LORD; I have spread out my hands to You." As in Madame Guyon's account, still the psalmist sought His God. Still he prayed and held his heart open to the presence of the Most High. Even when there seemed to be no response and no relief, he persevered in a disciplined way, every day—and there lies the key to survival.

Verse 10: "Will You perform wonders for the dead? Will the departed spirits rise and praise You?" Sarcasm and anger began to surface. Relentless and senseless pain and suffering sometimes reduce us to that. "So you want to be praised, Lord? How can I do that if I'm dead? Is that what you want?" I remained angry a long time, but the intensity of my own experience of suffering eventually burned that out of me and I learned to submit to whatever God might send or allow.

Verses 11–13: "Will Your lovingkindness be declared in the grave, Your faithfulness in Abaddon? Will Your wonders be made known in the darkness? And Your righteousness in the land of forgetfulness? But I, O Lord, have cried out to You for help, and in the morning my prayer comes before You." In other words, "No matter what I suffer, no matter how far away You seem to be and no matter how angry I may become at Your distance, Lord, yet I pray. I seek Your presence." For the sake of emphasis, I say again that perseverance plays a key role in surviving the dark night. Stay with the ministry. Keep serving Him. Maintain worship. Study the Word. Pray daily. Determine not to break your stride. When all seems such fog and blindness that you cannot see your hand before your face, choose, by an act of the will, to trust the eternal compass and walk on. Even if it feels all wrong, it will be right.

Verse 14: "O Lord, why do You reject my soul? Why do You hide Your face from me?" I repeat that the dark night is a time of perceived abandonment and even rejection, a season when God blesses by not blessing. Here lies the mystery of redemptive suffering and fear!

Verse 15: "I was afflicted and about to die from my youth on; I suffer Your terrors; I am overcome." For the psalmist, this had been going on for a long time. Too long. Even from adolescence. Suffering had worn him down and rendered him helpless before the onslaught of his pain.

Verses 16–17: "Your burning anger has passed over me; Your terrors have destroyed me. They have surrounded me like water all day long; they have encompassed me altogether." In other words, "I'm drowning. The water has gone over my head. I'm helpless. I'm dying. And You've done it, Lord.

You're responsible. You've brought this fear of mine out into the light and now it's out of control."

◊ Verse 18: "You have removed lover and friend far from me; my acquaintances are in darkness." Profound loneliness fills the dark night. No one understands. No one hears. Well-intentioned fools give shallow advice based on hurtful misunderstanding and shallow theology. To avoid the sting of their misguided wisdom, you begin to hide from people. Because those who suffer in this way are seldom any fun to be with, friendships gradually erode. In the face of their own powerlessness to help, people flee. And here we leave the psalmist, without friends, without hope and without praise. Knowing only that his gnawing hunger for God raged unabated, he maintained the discipline of seeking God daily, no matter how deaf or distant the heavens seemed.

What does this mean? What purpose does it serve? The answer is preparation. For many years God has been preparing for a new move of His Spirit. I believe it will take forms we have never seen before—or experienced too little of. It will not focus so much on signs and wonders as on the gentle compassion of Jesus and His mercy. Signs and wonders of an order never before seen will manifest, but these will be eclipsed by an even more important revival of the character of Jesus shining through His people.

This will be a revival in, of and for the church, more than just a wave that breaks and is gone again, but a time in which the Holy Spirit will descend and remain because of what God has done to prepare the foundation in His bride, and most especially her leadership. I believe a great many of us have been and are being prepared by means of what St. John of the Cross called the dark night of the soul. Madame Guyon spoke of it in the quote above. The author of Psalm 88 experienced it in his hurt and abandonment.

A new generation is emerging that I believe has been largely held back and hidden until now. Their leaders have been going to school, so to speak, and the day of graduation has arrived.

These leaders have been driven into the wilderness while everyone else was having fun. These have wept while others laughed, and lost out while others prospered. As confusing as this season has been, in that brokenness they have learned to love as Jesus loved. They have worked through a personal depth of sharing in the cross of Christ and His resurrection, becoming more one with Jesus both in His death and in His life than they had ever before understood or experienced.

Pathema

Pathema is a New Testament Greek word that means "suffering," but suffering of a particular kind, the suffering necessary to the calling. It means that if you would accept the calling, you must accept the suffering that comes with it as the price of attaining it. Those who refuse the suffering cannot attain the calling.

Some occurrences of *pathema* in Scripture (emphases added):

> For I consider that the *sufferings* of this present time are not worthy to be compared with the glory that is to be revealed to us.
>
> Romans 8:18

> For just as the *sufferings* of Christ are ours in abundance, so also our comfort is abundant through Christ. But if we are afflicted, it is for your comfort and salvation; or if we are comforted, it is for your comfort, which is effective in the patient enduring of the same *sufferings* which we also suffer; and our hope for you is firmly grounded, knowing that as you are sharers of our sufferings, so also you are sharers of our comfort.
>
> 2 Corinthians 1:5–7

> That I may know Him and the power of His resurrection and the fellowship of His *sufferings*, being conformed to His death.
>
> Philippians 3:10

Now I rejoice in my *sufferings* for your sake, and in my flesh I do my share on behalf of His body, which is the church, in filling up what is lacking in Christ's afflictions.

Colossians 1:24

Now you followed my teaching, conduct, purpose, faith, patience, love, perseverance, persecutions, and *sufferings*, such as happened to me at Antioch, at Iconium and at Lystra; what persecutions I endured, and out of them all the Lord rescued me!

2 Timothy 3:10–11

But we do see Him who was made for a little while lower than the angels, namely, Jesus, because of the *suffering* of death crowned with glory and honor, so that by the grace of God He might taste death for everyone. For it was fitting for Him, for whom are all things, and through whom are all things, in bringing many sons to glory, to perfect the author of their salvation through *sufferings*. For both He who sanctifies and those who are sanctified are all from one.

Hebrews 2:9–10

But remember the former days, when, after being enlightened, you endured a great conflict of *sufferings*.

Hebrews 10:32

Beloved, do not be surprised at the fiery ordeal among you, which comes upon you for your testing, as though some strange thing were happening to you; but to the degree that you share the *sufferings* of Christ, keep on rejoicing, so that also at the revelation of His glory you may rejoice with exultation.

1 Peter 4:12–13

Perhaps most important is 1 Peter 4:1–2: "Therefore, since Christ has suffered in the flesh, arm yourselves also with the same purpose, because he who has *suffered* in the flesh has ceased from sin, so as to live the rest of the time in the flesh no longer for the lusts of men, but for the will of God" (emphasis added).

Calling, Exile and Destiny

Scripture shows us a repeated pattern of life and destiny in which a man first receives a call to ministry or some high level of influence, experiences success, is driven into exile and then finally returns to fulfill his destiny in the Lord. *Pathema* is integral to the process. For example, God destined Joseph to lead his brothers (calling) and gave him powerful gifts of prophecy (success). Unbroken, arrogant and immature, he tried them out on his brothers and created such offense that they sold him into slavery (exile). Later, in Egypt, he rose to power, his true destiny (return), and used that position to minister to his family in a time of famine.

The prophet Samuel anointed David king (calling). Through military victory he achieved prominence in Saul's court and enjoyed the praise of the people (success), only to be driven into the wilderness by Saul's jealous insanity (exile). Yet it was he who, after Saul's death, united the tribes and established a stable monarchy (return). Destiny follows the dark night. The dark night of exile prepares the servant for destiny.

New Testament Saul, who later became Paul, was converted (calling) and immediately began preaching in Damascus, leading many to Christ (success), but fled the city under threat of death to spend fourteen years in Tarsus making tents (exile). Finally, the eldership of Antioch sent for him, and ultimately launched him on his missionary journeys (return).

In each case we see calling and initial success, followed by exile (wilderness) and then a return and entrance into true destiny. God summons us, gives us a taste of our gifting and then sends us to the crucible of suffering and exile where our character undergoes change and refinement. In the end, having been prepared by means of a baptism of extended fire, He calls us back to service and into our true destiny. The promised land always lies on the far side of a vast wilderness. After enjoying times of initial success and anointing, we leaders often undergo a wilderness exile of suffering in which we share the cross of Christ to a greater degree than the average Christian ever will. Each of us called in this way must in some form, or variety of forms, "[suffer] the loss of all things" in order that we may gain Christ (Philippians 3:8). Lacking the character it produces, those who refuse the cross cannot sustain the calling.

I once made the mistake of saying to an older prophetic friend that I thought ten years of suffering was long enough. He laughed at me in a fatherly way and in his Oklahoma southern drawl declared, "Ten years ain't nothin'! I been sufferin' twenty years. I like sufferin'! When I'm sufferin', then I get to be with Jesus!" I took it as a gentle slap in the face and pondered the truth of it for many years afterward.

We need a *lifestyle* of brokenness in which we take up our cross daily and follow Him—ultimately in restful joy and not in extended suffering—and we need the mercy of God for a revelation of His person and compassion that can only be attained on the other side of the cross. Like Paul in 1 Corinthians 2:2, because of the wilderness, I no longer care to know anything except Jesus Christ, and Him crucified.

Abiding in Him

There can be no more important lesson today than learning to abide in Jesus. The dark night teaches this most deeply and indelibly, revealing His nature to us and in us. It takes us out of ourselves and plants us in Him. Because of the dark night of the soul, I am no longer so much concerned with teaching the Body of Christ how to prophesy, heal, learn new truths or wield the gifts of the Spirit as I once was. It has all become so much simpler than that, and accepting titles like "prophet" or "apostle" or "healer" can be so distracting. Titles like these are often the match that lights the gasoline of ambition and pride. They frighten me. The goal must be to abide in Him, as opposed to abiding in ministry, or in manifestations of the Spirit, or in some kind of doctrine. In Jesus are hidden all the treasures.

A Sabbath Rest

In the dark night of the soul a certain man once asked the Lord how long the suffering had to go on, and the Lord replied, "Until there is nothing left to insult, nothing left to humiliate, nothing left to defend." Embrace what God sends and let it work. Do this with desperation because we desperately need it!

"So there remains a Sabbath rest for the people of God. For the one who has entered His rest has himself also rested from his works, as God did from His" (Hebrews 4:9–10). God must bring us to the end of our own works. In that kind of rest, He will do mighty and glorious things in our midst that we have never imagined, and it will seem to us just a natural walk with Jesus as we move in union with Him.

Out of this weakness created by God flows the true, clean and pure mercy of Jesus for which the lost and wounded hunger so desperately. We, in the end time church (if, in fact, these are the end times), must be a people of mercy above all else. Nothing else will do. Only the mercy of Jesus has the power to overcome and heal the overwhelming hurt and destruction this sinful world has brought upon itself.

Nine Purposes of the Dark Night of the Soul

When confronted with suffering, every Christian I have ever known has cried out to God, "Why!?" As the darkness deepens, the cries grow louder. Although the pain may continue unabated, just having a few answers can provide the strength to survive. For those who stay the course, such dark nights of the soul inevitably lead to outcomes every true believer desires.

One: *To abandon any hope of personal reward for loving or serving God.*

Luke 17:7–10 tells of the slave who receives no praise for merely obeying orders. Although we have been adopted as children of the house and are not slaves, it must be enough for us to know that we have obeyed our Lord, no matter the outcome, or apparent lack of it. So long as some hope of personal reward survives as a motivation for service, it will color what we do, how we do it and the kind of energy we invest in it. Service motivated by personal need must give way to service motivated by love for the One we serve.

Many of us have suffered at the hands of "prophets" who bring a good word, but they defile or abuse us in their delivery through their need for self-validation and recognition. We have seen those prophetic "healers" who, for the same reason, promise healing that never materializes—and all to be certain we continue to fill up their meetings and their offering plates. We recognize the foul reek of ambition and the need for adulation and praise that feeds it. God desires a generation of leaders and servants to hear and serve Him clearly and cleanly so they can speak and act accurately and compassionately in His name. He needs for us to value serving Him more than the thrill we get from doing it. *Pathema* with our Lord is the singular doorway to that resting place.

For those not in some form of ministry, can you imagine what might happen if a business were operated with elements of character in its mission statement? What if obedience to Christ governed business practices and treatment of employees no matter how those employees might treat us? Or what might happen if Christian employees served employers with the kind of heart the apostle taught?

> Slaves, be obedient to those who are your masters according to the flesh, with fear and trembling, in the sincerity of your heart, as to Christ; not by way of eyeservice, as men-pleasers, but as slaves of Christ, doing the will of God from the heart. With good will render service, as to the Lord, and not to men.
>
> Ephesians 6:5–7

In each of these scenarios, we must learn to obey God for the sheer pleasure of knowing we obeyed. Let that be our reward. The dark night renders powerless the appeal of any other motivation.

Two: To expose and purify defects by breaking them.

The dark night of the soul will expose everything about you as defective. You will appear stripped of every virtue. Paul wrote: "For I know that nothing good dwells in me, that is, in my flesh; for the willing is present in me, but the doing of the good is not" (Romans 7:18). We are not basically good people who somehow got broken and are going to be fixed by Jesus. We are thoroughly sinful people who must be crucified with Him and then raised to new life. There can be no other remedy.

Several times during my own dark night I found myself embroiled in a situation in which I had to make a choice, but no matter what choice I made, I would appear to have broken my word to someone. No matter what move I made, I could not act with apparent integrity. I felt trapped, stripped of virtue, and I could do nothing about it. God allowed me to be maneuvered into such positions because I had to realize that in my flesh without His help I could not even guard my basic integrity. Like the apostle Paul, I had to come to despise every sense of self-goodness I had ever borne so that

I could receive His. I learned that everything I had ever done or produced had been tainted with sin in some way. "Nothing good dwells in me" (Romans 7:18). I would walk in His righteousness, not my own.

Three: To bring about abandonment and despair of self.

The dark night enables a complete and accurate assessment of your own total depravity that sharply accents the depth and magnitude of God's grace to cover it. When you have accepted and confessed the true depth of your sin, no accusation leveled at you can have any real force. You become unassailably secure, at rest in the totality of the forgiveness and grace you have been given. "There is now no condemnation for those who are in Christ Jesus" (Romans 8:1). When you know your condition and understand God's grace in relation to it, nothing remains to be threatened. You can fully rest in Him only when you have despaired of yourself.

Four: To bring about a faith without agenda or demand of God by means of surrendering every dream and hope.

The apostle Paul had learned to be content in all circumstances (see Philippians 4:11). It all pays the same, whether I stand before a thousand or ten, whether rich or poor, imprisoned or free. It must be the same joy, whether I play my music for five thousand or for a coffeehouse audience of two. Or will I follow Him if my problems refuse to evaporate? Am I His even if my dreams all fail? Will I serve and obey Him even if no prophetic word spoken over my life ever comes to pass? Or is it all somehow conditional? Is God blessing me only when things go well, or is His blessing equally present when the world seems to be crashing down around my ears? Can I have the faith to see and understand that mystery? Are they His dreams or mine? Does He own them, or do I? Is it flesh? Or Spirit?

Five: To bring to rest the higher functions of the spirit.

The higher functions of the spirit (human spirit) include ease of movement in the Holy Spirit, hearing God, perceiving Him, and Jesus shining in and through us. In the flesh, these functions suffer coloration by personal agendas and desires as we try to manipulate God to obtain what we think we need. Manipulation flows from unbelief that God will really honor His promise to provide. Pure hearing comes only in and through the presence of faith in the absence of personal agenda or demand.

This failure to rest in the higher functions of the spirit leads us to adopt errant theologies as we seek methods and procedures that we believe will compel God to act on our behalf. For instance, much of what passes as prosperity teaching in the current day has its root in the quest to manipulate God's principles to achieve a desired end. It appeals to us because we have not come to rest either in His Spirit or in ours. In the end this boils down to a thinly disguised version of salvation by works. We have not yet learned real faith. The same could be said of methods of prayer, many approaches to healing ministry and flesh-based efforts at learning to hear God. When the higher functions of the spirit have been brought to rest, these things flow naturally and smoothly.

Six: To bring about a love for God that passes beyond loving Him for what He has done or will do for us.

We need to develop a love for God that passes beyond the reward we get from feeling it. Do I love God because it feels good to do so, because of what He has done for me, or do I love Him for His own sake? To love because it feels good to love constitutes use and abuse in any relationship. Real love perseveres even when love involves suffering. Do any of us really believe that Jesus felt all warm and mushy about going to the cross? Loving us felt pretty bad that night in Gethsemane, worse when the scourging began, still worse when the nails pierced His hands and feet. True love goes beyond any return we might get for doing it.

The dark night brings us to the end of, "I love You, God, because. . ." It teaches us a love for God that loves Him when we have no strength left to love and when we perceive nothing of His touch. This love reaches deeper and ultimately produces a greater satisfaction than the conditional kind that so many believers seem to hold in their hearts. The psalmist in Psalm 88 reached out to God morning by morning in love, even in the midst of despair.

Seven: To bring about a purity of fellowship with Him.

"That I may know Him and the power of His resurrection and the fellowship of His sufferings" (Philippians 3:10). One's closest friends will always be those who have stood by in hard times. Most of my current church staff, for instance, have been with me ten years or more. Many of those years have been exceedingly difficult ones. As we have shared extended seasons of suffering together for the ministry, our love for one another has grown. We have come to know and appreciate one another at greater depths than we possibly could have under any other circumstances.

The same simple truth applies to the suffering of the dark night of the soul and its effect on our relationship with Jesus. How could we know Him fully without sharing at some level the depth of what He suffered? How could we understand the true power of His resurrection—and our own—without experiencing in some way both His death and His resurrection? "For if we have become united with Him in the likeness of His death, certainly we shall also be in the likeness of His resurrection" (Romans 6:5).

Eight: To find humility.

Humility brings about defenselessness, based on security in Jesus, leading to vulnerability and transparency. In burnout, for instance, I concealed myself at least in part to protect my pride as well as to prevent further wounding, but in the dark night I learned to allow my sins and weaknesses to show. I could openly admit them, even before crowds of people, because I no longer needed to defend all those tender places inside of me by creating the illusion of strength or puffing myself up with delusions of grandeur. Since then, people seem to sense the openness. As I became more transparent and vulnerable, people no longer tended to use what I shared against me, but sensed instead that I am with them, not regarding myself as above them.

As a result, although I would never foolishly make a claim to having achieved humility, I do know that I seldom hear accusations of arrogance. Prior to the dark night, such accusations frequently came my way—and rightly so.

Nine: To discover radical compassion.

Radical compassion takes root because you can at last truly identify with sinners, having been made to face and accept your own failure. The dark night brings about cross-centered, compelling compassion. The dark night destroys judgmentalism in every form and in every root.

In my own case, I recall believing myself to be a kind man and experiencing confusion when people told me that was not so. In truth, I secretly despised those who suffered chronic pain or who experienced overwhelming difficulties in overcoming life's obstacles. Relentless and overpowering suffering taught me lessons in human weakness that I could have learned in no other way.

10

THE NEW LEADERSHIP

For most of my life since the Charismatic Renewal impacted my family in 1958 (I was seven years old when my parents brought it home), much focus has been placed on learning new tools for ministry, new truths and new ways to be personally healed or made more whole. Too much emphasis fell on self-improvement and personal fulfillment, often reflecting the values of a self-centered society more than loving God, being loved by Him or loving His people.

As a result, we rather lost ourselves in the gifts of the Spirit, as if those gifts formed the focal point of our Christian life, rather than the reality, the nature and the presence of Jesus. Many of us saw our gifts as the measure of our individual significance among God's people, using our gifts as platforms to further our personal kingdoms and ambitions, and until very recently it seemed God allowed us to get away with it. His grace does cover a multitude of sins—up to a point.

If we would fully participate in the dawning glory, however, we must understand more deeply than we ever have that the gifts of the Spirit exalt Jesus and His nature, not us. They are tools for delivering His compassion to the needy, the broken and the lost and for building up others in the Body of Christ, not the means of our personal exaltation.

The longer I live, the more convinced I am that true compassion flows consistently only from a broken spirit and a contrite heart (see Psalm 51:17), and that a broken spirit and a contrite heart are most often brought about through a wilderness of redemptive suffering, a dark night of the soul. Only the broken and contrite heart can fully, wisely and most effectively use the tools.

Redemptive Suffering

Unfortunately, the modern church has largely lost the concept of redemptive suffering. Society conditions us to regard suffering in any form as illegal, and we spend millions of dollars annually trying to anesthetize it medically. As a result, we too often teach that all pain is of the devil and therefore must be avoided or cast out, but this teaching is culturally conditioned, rather than biblically sound. It fails to represent the whole counsel of God, either in Scripture or in the experience of the saints and martyrs throughout history.

Some forms of suffering come from the hand of God to bring about brokenness in His servants, to put the flesh to death and to create rested dependence on Him, humility and wisdom. This kind of suffering must be embraced, cherished and accepted in the faith that it leads to a greater glory.

As I mentioned in the last chapter, when speaking of His own sufferings, Paul often used the Greek word *pathema*. *Pathema* must be embraced as part of the inevitable price, the *sine qua non* of high calling, and I speak not only of high calling in the church. God has strategically placed highly gifted people in every walk of life to influence the culture around us and to demonstrate the power of His Kingdom in the public arena. High calling in the Lord extends beyond the roles we traditionally regard as Christian vocations. Whether God deploys you in the church or in the secular world, His preparation for high calling remains the same.

Paul used *pathema*, for instance, in Philippians 3:10 when He spoke of knowing not only the power of the Lord's resurrection but also "the fellowship of His sufferings." Oneness with Jesus can never be complete apart from sharing the fullness of His experience, which includes redemptive suffering. One does not accept the calling of God to discipleship without at the same time accepting the price of that calling. Pray as you may, God will do nothing to relieve *pathema* until it produces what He intends it to produce. To relieve *pathema* prematurely would be to cheat both us and His Kingdom of the benefit.

In short, if you want to play football, you must run the laps. If you wish to earn the scholarship, you must choose to study. Similarly, God's servants pay a price in redemptive suffering for the glory of sharing in the compassionate nature of Jesus and the exercise of His power. But unlike skill in competitive sports, we cannot "achieve" *pathema*. We can only embrace and submit to it, letting it do its work in us. We gain the compassion of Jesus not through human effort but only by submitting to and sharing in the death of Jesus in order that we might attain His life.

The Price of High Calling

Those appointed for high calling in these present days must therefore undergo some form of wilderness, or dark night of the soul, brought about by the hand of God. Most often this will be marked, at least in part, by a profound awareness of individual human failure and the grief brought on by that newfound understanding.

For instance, on the night before the crucifixion—and rather full of himself—Peter, the apostle-in-training, boasted that he would die with Jesus if necessary. A few hours later, when the soldiers came to Gethsemane to arrest his Lord, Peter acted on his boast. Ready to die gloriously as a warrior fighting by Jesus' side, he drew a sword and struck at the servant of the high priest, only to receive Jesus' rebuke.

Later that same night, brave Peter three times denied that he had ever known the Lord. Although he understood the honor of dying in battle, the prospect of death on a cross and sharing the humiliation and shame of it reduced him to cowardice. The wonder of redemption meant that before Peter could lead effectively in power with the heart and nature of his Lord, he had to realize not his strength but his weakness and his desperate need for a Savior.

The night before the crucifixion was a test I believe God actually intended Peter to fail. "Simon, Simon, behold, Satan has demanded permission to sift you like wheat; but I have prayed for you, that your faith may not fail; and you, when once you have turned again, strengthen your brothers" (Luke 22:31–32). Paradoxically, his failure qualified him to lead.

Those who have embraced their own weakness have been freed to walk in the good, clean strength of the Lord. Out of Peter's failure, compassion flowed to strengthen his brothers. Power and authority settle best upon a bed of compassion arising from brokenness of spirit, which is simply the failure of confidence in things human.

Many Called, Few Chosen

Jesus said that many are called but few are chosen (see Matthew 22:14). If salvation comes by faith alone and not by works, then what makes the difference between the called and the chosen? Are only a few destined to be saved? The answer lies in the three main groups of people who surrounded Jesus in His earthly ministry. First came the multitude. Although imperfectly, they believed in Jesus, and by reason of that faith, they were saved. Their faith arose from a desperate need for healing and deliverance and from their perception that Jesus could meet these needs. Figuratively speaking, they played the part of consumers in His ministry, following after Him only because He sold a product for which they felt a hunger. They believed in Him because He met their personal needs better than anything else currently available to them.

After the multitude came the seventy identified in Scripture as disciples. They followed Jesus wherever He went and eventually embarked on a missionary journey, sent out by Him two by two (see Luke 10). They followed Him because He had chosen and called them to serve, rather than to consume—and they had responded. Active participation as a minister rather than as a consumer differentiates the disciple from the multitude.

Finally, Jesus called the twelve who became apostles to be closest to Him and destined them to play key roles in the later development of the church. Their proximity to Him equipped them for a much greater exercise of authority than the seventy. They would eventually lead and mold the church as it infiltrated every society they could reach.

The point? Jesus calls many to become disciples, as opposed to mere members of the multitude, but few actually respond. This is not to say that those who fail to choose the higher calling lose their salvation. When God calls a man or woman to become more than a consumer, more than just a believer among the multitude, when He calls him or her to a higher calling to serve and lead others, He subjects that person to a training program designed to expose and break every fleshly confidence and hidden sin. This is the dark night of the soul. Not mere burnout. Not just exhaustion. It goes deeper than burnout or exhaustion and requires an embracing of the wilderness untainted by anger or rebellion.

Few are chosen because many abort the process in anger or despair before it can run its course. The price in suffering seems too high to pay. Those who opt out to rejoin the multitude remain saved and redeemed because faith in Jesus assures the fact of their salvation, no matter what its level or intensity, but the loss of destiny and the aimlessness that results from such an abandonment of calling are grievous things to see. Those who will not take the cross cannot accept the calling.

A Profile of the Chosen and Refined

In our day, God has long been refining a generation of leaders and servants in the crucible of brokenness, in the dark night of their souls. If you have been included as one of these, a general profile may apply to you. You have felt in your heart, perhaps for a long time, that God has some great thing for you to do, and maybe the early days of your ministry or your worldly employment were powerfully anointed and successful, but for some time now you have been held back. Often, you have been forced to watch from the sidelines while others with less gifting or wisdom than your own have been blessed, promoted and prospered. You have agonized over the question of why. Wounded and feeling left out, even rejected, you have then condemned yourself for the jealousy you know to be illegal.

Disaster has been a dominant theme for months, even years. Major setbacks have piled one upon another. Disappointment threatens to crush the life and drive the hope from your heart and spirit. Or perhaps you simply carry a burden of desperate hurt and agonizing loneliness that seems to have no cause or reason. Your dark night may be characterized more by an inner desolation than by any outward or measurable set of circumstances. From the heart of this desolation, you have tearfully and perhaps angrily wondered where God is. Even your prayers seem to go nowhere. All these things may appear on the surface to be burnout symptoms, but this goes much deeper.

It may be that those known for the accuracy of their words have prophesied great things over you, but the only prophecies that have come to pass for you have been those predicting disaster. Confused and hurt by this, you have cried out, "Why has the Lord dealt with me in this way?" He has dealt with you in this way because first He issues the promise and then He begins the preparation. The heart of it is brokenness.

It would have been a tremendous help if someone somewhere among God's people had given you a theological grid for understanding your experience, but our contemporary faith has been too conditioned by the values and demands of the pagan society in which we live. In the eyes of the church, your experience of suffering is illegal, of the devil. No one ever told you that your call to discipleship would be a blessing preceded by a crucifixion—to be followed by a resurrection.

Why?

Why is such a crushing so necessary? Because our own strength, what we have known in the past, cannot sustain us in the glory into which God is leading us. To cope with the increasing depth of destruction rising around us in the world we must reach, we need a transcendent level of compassion, and a sense of peace under fire that cannot be threatened. To save, heal and disciple a multitude of this world's lost, we need a "loaves and fishes" kind of multiplication of the compassion and power of Jesus. Our pitifully and woefully inadequate offering of service will need to be miraculously multiplied by the hand of God.

The Limitations of Natural Capacity

No matter how great the talent, ability or intelligence, in the unbroken believer the natural capacity of the individual limits and restricts the flow of God's compassion and power. When Paul pled for God to heal the affliction that kept him weak, God answered, "My grace is sufficient for you, for power is perfected in weakness" (2 Corinthians 12:9). Our natural selves are completely inadequate for the task of ministry or for the glory set before us, but in the weakness in which God perfects His power, Jesus multiplies what little we can offer and glorifies Himself far beyond what we could have produced on our own. In godly brokenness, grace and power flow unhindered and unlimited by the flesh.

The Need for Wholeness and Holiness

Furthermore, our present level of holiness cannot adequately sustain the glory to come. God's glory and anointing are a blessing, but also a weight and pressure needing a solid foundation on which to rest. As the anointing increases, so does the spiritual pressure that tests and strains our character. Accountability therefore rises with the anointing. The weight of God's anointing resting on a person must ultimately force open and reveal every crack and fissure in his or her inner self, every unholy ambition, every self-seeking impulse, every control mechanism, every unhealthy need, every immorality.

At first, God exposes our inner condition only to ourselves, but if we turn away, seeking to avoid or deny His dealings, then our Lord makes our issues public. I could include a long list of cases we would all recognize in which, as a last resort, God went public with a prominent leader's hidden sin to break him and draw him home again. Given a choice between saving a ministry and saving a person, our Lord will choose the person every time, so intensely does He love and desire us. In His mercy and by means of the crucible of the cross, God exposes our sin to cleanse and humble us so that, under the weight of the glory to come, we will be able to stand.

For everyone who does evil hates the Light, and does not come to the Light for fear that his deeds will be exposed. But he who practices the truth comes to the Light, so that his deeds may be manifested as having been wrought in God.

John 3:20–21

In the days to come we will need holiness of the heart and a deeper river of compassion to strengthen us to stand in the wondrous places our Lord will take us. For this reason, God has been grinding many of His chosen vessels to powder so fine it will float on water, as I once heard a well-known prophetic minister declare. He went on to point out that crushed limestone, when moistened with the water of the Holy Spirit, results in concrete. Weakness becomes strength.

Strength in Weakness

Our wise and compassionate God therefore leads us into the mystery of the experience of the apostle Paul.

Because of the surpassing greatness of the revelations, for this reason, to keep me from exalting myself, there was given me a thorn in the flesh, a messenger of Satan to torment me—to keep me from exalting myself! Concerning this I implored the Lord three times that it might leave me. And He has said to me, "My grace is sufficient for you, for power is perfected in weakness." Most gladly, therefore, I will rather boast about my weaknesses, so that the power of Christ may dwell in me. Therefore I am well content with weaknesses, with insults, with distresses, with persecutions, with difficulties, for Christ's sake; for when I am weak, then I am strong.

2 Corinthians 12:7–10

To those conditioned by the health, wealth and prosperity gospel arising out of the materialistic society in which we live, these verses might seem impenetrable, "was given me," Paul's phrase quoted in the passage above, is in the "divine passive" in the original Greek, meaning that God Himself gave the thorn, the messenger of Satan, to Paul to accomplish and maintain a state of weakness and brokenness in His servant.

Paradoxically, by leaving Paul weak and unhealed, by placing him in a position that forced him to trust, God magnified the power He was able to pour through him in ministry to others and even in ministry to Paul personally. "When I am weak, then I am strong." No matter how talented or brilliant the minister, that which is limited by the flesh can never match what flows freely in the Spirit. Three times Paul cried out for healing and three times God refused. It was not that his faith was insufficient or that he carried any obvious sin. God needed a broken vessel through whom to pour His miracles of loaves and fishes, multiplying His mercy for thousands who would hear Paul's message and receive his ministry. And He needed someone who would remain utterly humble through it all.

If an unbroken Paul had been allowed power in himself, he would have been full of himself and full of ambition, striving and control, rather than full of Jesus. The result would not have been true faith, but an abusive personality cult.

Confronted by the Holiness Mirror

I myself thought that as I grew older in the Lord and grew closer to Him, I would feel ever holier, cleaner and stronger. Holier and cleaner I have definitely felt, but I have become deeply aware of how incomplete I am apart from Him, how broken and destroyed by sin. The result has not been discouragement or heaviness. Instead, I have been filled with a growing and joyous awareness of the infinite magnitude of God's grace toward me. This is a place in which I can rest.

In the midst of watching my life fall apart, God began to hold me up to the "holiness mirror." The holiness mirror seems to be positioned about two inches from the end of my nose so that, no matter which way I turn, I cannot escape being confronted with my own reflection. In brokenness, God makes us face ourselves.

Gazing into that mirror I realized that for most of my ministry I had been full of myself and that, while in that state, God's grace and mercy insured that not one prophetic promise anyone ever spoke over my personal life came to pass—unless it involved suffering. I could not have sustained His destiny for me had it been built on my cracked foundation. If I had achieved the success and acclaim promised by those prophetic words before *pathema* had done its work, I would have patted myself on the back and gone off to teach others how to manipulate the principles of God to obtain spiritual success. Jesus wanted something better, something more truly reflective of His nature.

God has never been about manipulating principles. He perfects His power in weakness. Trained in weakness and brokenness, the new leadership will therefore be immeasurably powerful. They will lead boldly when Jesus leads boldly, rather than operate from selfish ambition or the need for self-validation. Their heart's cry will be nothing more than to be with Jesus, doing what Jesus does as He does it. Only the powerless can truly be empowered.

Power in Powerlessness

In this new generation of compassionate shepherds and leaders, God must remove ambition, hunger for power, religion, legalism, control mechanisms, unbelief and judgment, most of which are deeply hidden in subtle ways and places. In my case, all my life, personal strength has been important to me. As I noted previously, my Osage Indian ancestors worshiped strength and size. Strength is written into my genetic code at levels so deep I have trouble separating myself from it. In my flesh I naturally long for and seek emotional, physical and spiritual strength. Until the dark night of the soul did its work, a quest for power had consumed most of my life and infected everything I did.

I grew up in a power atmosphere. My father pastored before me. As far as I know, we were the first family to come into the charismatic renewal in our old mainline denomination in 1958. Instances of the supernatural seemed to be the soup in which I lived. Things like demonic deliverance happened regularly in our living room when I was just a small boy. During my childhood years, miraculous emotional and physical healings seemed normal to me.

My most vivid memory of my father in prayer is of walking past his room late one night and hearing him inside blissfully praying in tongues loudly enough for the sound to come through his closed door. As a child, I coveted that gift, not because I thought it would bring me into a new intimacy with God, but because it represented power to me at a time when the world made me feel powerless.

Later, as an adult with seven years of higher education under my belt, I tried to build a strong church and a powerful ministry. Cultivating a dominant persona, I hungered for personal strength and spiritual power to heal, to teach, to lead and to persuade.

A fleshly dynamo, a driven man, I secretly felt contempt for those unable to keep pace with me. In the spirit, however, I experienced little of the power of God personally—none of the overwhelming experiences of which so many others testified. Others fell down under the power of the Spirit, but not me. Others shook or laughed, but not me. Others sensed the Spirit of God through me, but I always felt personally cheated, jealous of those who did experience those things.

One day in the midst of whining over my lack of that kind of experience, the Lord confronted me with one of the more portentous questions of my life. *Which would you rather have? Foolish power or powerful wisdom?* Having read of

King Solomon, I knew the answer and rightly chose wisdom, but I was a fool. I was a fool not because the choice was not right (it was), but because I had no clue what price the getting of wisdom would exact from me. Knowledge comes from study, but ultimately wisdom comes only through suffering. God has been training up a generation of wise leaders, but even as I came to understand the price of my choice, I found myself even more a fool because I failed to recognize that when my strength and arrogance had been broken, I would still be a fool. I would just be a fool for Him.

God then asked, *Would you be willing to be the cause of healing and wholeness for many if no one ever knew it was you?* Would I be willing to set others in motion and see them praised for what I started? I said yes, and answered rightly, because I knew what was expected of me, but again I was a fool. I was a fool because again I was blind to the full meaning of the question and what the lesson would cost me while I learned it. Death would be the price. I would have to let go, but only by having my fingers slowly and painfully pried from the controls of my life and ministry, one at a time, by Someone a great deal stronger than I am. More importantly, I would have to learn to rest in my powerlessness.

Reprise: the Holiness Mirror

When I had finally become too weak to argue or maintain my defenses, when life's nightmare and the Lord's apparent absence had taken their toll, God began to show me the truth about myself. I came to understand that if my Lord did not graciously reduce me to a weakness like Paul's, and if He did not keep me in that state, I would never see what He wanted me to see. Strong in myself, I would be blind.

I thought I had been building God's Kingdom, but I saw that I had been pursuing success and running on ambition, using the Spirit of God to advance my personal agenda, building my own ministry. I thought I had been challenging people to serve God, but in reality I served the god of my self-validation, manipulating people to worship the idol of my selfish ambition. I mouthed glory to God, but I hungered to be seen.

"Lord, I just want to serve You!" I cried, protesting my innocence, "Why is all this evil happening to me?"

Yes, but you also want to be important, so you serve yourself.

"Lord, I only want to minister to people and see them healed." That one was marvelously pious and—I thought—true.

Yes, but you also want to feel My power as a means to validate yourself and you want the people to be healed and "behave" so that you can look good.

"Lord, I just want the people to evangelize," I muttered as my protests began to lose their punch.

Yes, but you also want the biggest church in town so you can feel secure. And you are angry when I do not cooperate!

I could not understand why my friends, who had built the church with me, wanted to leave me, or why my congregation had apparently become so lifeless. In my weakness, I came to see my own responsibility, that I had driven people away with my intensity, ambition and controlling nature born of unbelief. The revelation of my dysfunction devastated me, the more so because I knew that no matter how hard I tried, I could not make myself change. The patterns were too deeply ingrained and I had been subconsciously reinforcing them for much too long. I did not know the difference between the real me and the persona I had constructed for public viewing. I needed to die, and God Himself intervened to make it happen.

A Sabbath Rest

God will not grant a new accumulation of knowledge and then let that become the focus of this generation of leaders but will rather forge our character in the crucible of the cross, which is death leading to life, the broken heart and spirit He does not despise (see Psalm 51:17). Purified motives make purified and powerful lives and ministries. Purified motives come only from brokenness. When I am weak, then He is strong.

"So there remains a Sabbath rest for the people of God. For the one who has entered His rest has himself also rested from his works, as God did from His" (Hebrews 4:9–10). God brings us to the end of our own works, and of our own ways of doing His works. In and through the Sabbath rest of the broken heart and spirit, He will do mighty things.

> Therefore, since Christ has suffered in the flesh, arm yourselves also with the same purpose, because he who has suffered in the flesh has ceased from sin, so as to live the rest of the time in the flesh no longer for the lusts of men, but for the will of God.
>
> 1 Peter 4:1–2

Out of this weakness whose true name is strength flows the clean and pure mercy of Jesus for which the lost and wounded hunger so desperately.

11

THE WILDERNESS

We live in a culture that conditions us to avoid suffering at all costs. We therefore have no paradigm for dealing with it, no framework by which to process it. Suffering frightens us. After initial demonstrations of compassion, even the church, which should be the agent of mercy, often retreats in fear from those who suffer relentlessly and inexplicably. Condemnation of the sufferer usually follows close behind. You had too little faith. You were in sin. You have not prayed hard enough, worked hard enough or given enough. These disasters came to you because of you. You are reaping something you have sown.

Because of our fearful inability to deal constructively with the wilderness experience, we often reject it, but in the Bible the wilderness plays an essential role in the lives and callings of God's people as an indispensable prerequisite for truly high calling. Jesus Himself underwent a wilderness testing before being released into His earthly ministry. Prophets and apostles passed through forms of personal wilderness that prepared them for their destinies. The whole nation of Israel, in fact, wandered forty years in the desert to be trained in readiness to take the Promised Land. They had been given a high calling as a people, but unbelief stood in the way. They still thought like slaves—Egypt loomed too large in their experience—but God needed a free people to take the land of Canaan. The character and integrity of Israel as a nation needed to be refined and cleansed before they would have the faith to take the Promised Land or the strength to sustain its blessing.

God must deal deeply with the character and integrity of the one He calls, stripping away fleshly structures to expose places of unbelief. I still marvel that through all the devastations and near disasters God allowed to come into my life, He never allowed me to slip. No matter how bad things looked or felt, I can see with 20/20 hindsight that He held me firmly, preserved and kept me. I have seen the goodness, the greater purpose, emerge, and I have entered into the faith and trust for which I had always longed. Not that I do not have to fight sometimes to retain what I have gained! I must choose the victory and stand firm in it.

We have come into a period in history when nothing will suffice for the character of those who lead but the true heart and nature of Jesus for His people. That nature never abuses, never manipulates and never violates. The root of all spiritual and ecclesiastical abuse is unbelief, personal insecurity and the need for self-validation. If I do not trust God for my place and position in this world, if my sense of His favor upon me stands in question, if I fear personal rejection, then I will seek to build a world of control or achievement around my flaws to anesthetize my feelings and to cover up my tender places. Sooner or later I will badly use both people and the church to accomplish place, position and self-protection.

Until the deep reaches of the heart of insecurity and un-belief have been broken—with its structures of control and ambition—none of us can safely wield the power of God or walk in the fullness of His calling. God established the wilderness as the place of suffering and loss designed to accomplish this brokenness in the hidden depths.

The Wilderness in Psalm 63

In Psalm 63:1, from the wilderness of Judah, King David cried out, "O God, You are my God; I shall seek You earnestly." Not, "I shall seek the latest techniques of spiritual warfare to defeat my enemy." Not, "I shall find out how to multiply the nation." Not, "How do I increase my power?" Not, "How do I overcome adversity or increase my prosperity?" but, "I shall seek You earnestly."

Wilderness fire consumes our personal agendas until we cease to see God as a means to an end and have been reduced at last to just one hunger, one longing: "My soul thirsts for You, my flesh yearns for You, in a dry and weary land where there is no water" (verse 1).

Paraphrased, David cried, "I can find no refreshment in this desert. I can no longer even sense Your presence, Lord. So hungry am I for You that the longing of my soul has become a thing felt even in the flesh of my body. Please, Lord, just let me be with You. Nothing else matters."

The next sentence is worded very curiously: "Thus I have seen You in the sanctuary, to see Your power and Your glory" (verse 2). Again paraphrased, David declared, "*Because* I have been in the desert, *because* I am thirsty and weary and broken, I have beheld You." Not through prosperity or success or power, but through the experience of the desert in the absence of prosperity, success or power, David beheld his God. *The wilderness strips away every ambition, every accomplishment, every ability of the flesh to achieve, every sinful habit of the heart, until nothing remains but a desperate craving hunger for the presence of Jesus.* Then, when no other hunger competes for attention, the revelation comes. The wilderness makes you simple and pure and sets you at rest with your God.

"Because Your lovingkindness is better than life, my lips will praise You" (verse 3). In the wilderness you despair of life. Success, building a great church, getting promoted at work, being recognized for what you do or being adored by your wife or husband all fade to insignificance next to longing after God. His lovingkindness, His touch and His presence become your singular consuming hunger.

Verse 5 declares, "My soul is satisfied as with marrow and fatness, and my mouth offers praises with joyful lips," as if to say, "I am weary. I am hungry. Thirsty. Alone. I have nothing, but have become rich. I am fulfilled, reduced to just one need, one hunger, and so I have beheld my God as I could never have beheld Him before. It is enough for me."

Verse 8 reads, "My soul clings to You." For all his kingly power, like a frightened and helpless child David clung tightly to his God. After the wilderness, more than ever before, he knew he was just a man—not powerful, not wise and not important. Without strength, defenseless and broken, his soul clung to the Lord, no longer concerned with power, wisdom or importance, but with only the embrace of his God.

At this point real faith comes. "But those who seek my life to destroy it, will go into the depths of the earth. They will be delivered over to the power of the sword; they will be a prey for foxes. But the king will rejoice in God" (verses 9–11). David would rejoice not in how mighty he had become, and not in all the right decisions he had made or the prosperity that had come to him, but in God alone. The wilderness had broken through layers of mistrust and unbelief to expose and cleanse his fear. Restfully now, he knew his God would fight for him, provide for him and do good for him.

Extended wilderness deprivation, loneliness, hunger, wandering and emptiness put you in touch with the only hunger that ever really matters. Because the wilderness crucifies all other desires but to be with your God, it makes you a safe leader who will not abuse, whether you lead in your church, in the world or at home. The wilderness prepares you to walk safely in destiny and blessing without polluting it with sin or human agenda.

God may delay your destiny, your life's blessing and your fulfillment (a mate, a calling, the place of your anointing, what you were created to do, your prosperity) because He knows you would trash it at this stage in your development. Your character has not yet been prepared to sustain the weight of it, so He holds the blessing in trust against that day when the wilderness has done its work.

In Ezekiel 34 the prophet railed against the shepherds who took advantage of the sheep and used the flock for their own benefit. In verse 10 he declared, "Thus says the LORD GOD, 'Behold, I am against the shepherds, and I will demand My sheep from them and make them cease from feeding sheep. So the shepherds will not feed themselves anymore, but I will deliver My flock from their mouth, so that they will not be food for them.'"

I believe a great many current leaders of the flock will be relieved of their duties in the days to come so that Jesus can give the flock into the care of other leaders who follow after His own heart and not after their own ambitions. Already we have witnessed a rising number of national leaders being exposed and removed from places of influence. A generation of wilderness-trained shepherds, men and women who have walked the dark night of the soul and come out the other side, will soon emerge and bring a new-old thing to the Body of Christ. He is training a people to walk with these leaders, a people who together will look like Him, who will be that bride that brings honor to His name, in all her glory without spot or wrinkle.

Wilderness Functions

Israel at its best cherished the wilderness. It could be a place of suffering for purification as well as a place to be gloriously

157

alone with God. In either case, just as the dark night of the soul serves the purposes of the Almighty for our good, so God leads us into the wilderness with specific purposes in mind. As a burnout victim or simply as one destined for higher calling, you have been led into the wilderness to prepare you for greater glory. Embrace it and live!

A Place of Testing

You shall remember all the way which the LORD your God has led you in the wilderness these forty years, that He might humble you, testing you, to know what was in your heart, whether you would keep His commandments or not. He humbled you and let you be hungry, and fed you with manna which you did not know, nor did your fathers know, that He might make you understand that man does not live by bread alone, but man lives by everything that proceeds out of the mouth of the LORD.

Deuteronomy 8:2–3

Will you stand firm with the Lord in the midst of the humbling and testing of your heart? No matter what might befall you, will you love Him? serve Him? praise Him? Will you do it no matter how your situation looks? No matter how dry or distant He seems? Whether things go right or wrong? The truth is that if you cannot stand for and with Him when everything seems wrong, then how shallow and cheap will your service be in the midst of blessing and prosperity?

After the wilderness, you no longer argue with God. A key part of the test is whether, under the worst of circumstances, you will keep His commandments. You no longer ask, "Does obedience work?" Whether you can perceive that it works or not, you obey simply for the sake of being with Him. Wilderness stripping and wilderness testing establish your faith on a base of pure hunger for the Lord and His will, without dispute or compromise. Make a place in your theology for long periods of failure and humiliation designed to break down interior walls that hinder intimacy with Him.

God will humiliate you in the very areas He plans to bless you, to prepare you for the blessing. Today I serve New Song Fellowship in Denver, Colorado, a growing multi-staff church in an area of the city where, until very recently, every church plant but us has failed. My international ministry has expanded. I enjoy favor everywhere I go in all that I do, but humiliation came before exaltation.

I am a gifted musician and songwriter, but in Idaho in the 1980s the music remained shut off and hidden. I came to Denver on the promise of release but instead endured some ridicule by fellow musicians in the megachurch where I served as executive pastor for fourteen months. Most doors seemed closed. New Song now owns its own recording studio, and we have become known for the power and glory of our worship.

I guard my integrity with my life, but at the first church I served in Denver, my honor was trashed, my integrity questioned and slanderous lies were spread concerning me. Now God vindicates me wherever I go.

Are you called as a prophet? No one wants to hear your words. You are not even very accurate at first. You see yourself as a teacher? No one attends your class. God has destined your family for blessing? Then why does everything seem so wrong all the time? You are a businessman gifted for prosperity? Right now you are broke and nothing you do succeeds as it should! We must be reduced to a state in which we receive honor and humiliation with equal gratitude because we have been reduced to a singular and purified hunger for the presence and the love of Jesus.

A Place Where You Learn Who You Are

In the desert you learn who you are and become established in it. In Matthew 3 and 4 Jesus came up from the waters of baptism only to be driven immediately into the wilderness by the Holy Spirit to be tempted by the devil. Those called of God will be tempted by the devil in ways God Himself actually commissions. In Matthew 4:3 and 4:6 Satan challenged Jesus, "If You are the Son of God…" The key word is *if*. Satan sought an exploitable window of insecurity or doubt in Jesus concerning His identity. Jesus' answers firmly established that He would do and say nothing but what He saw and heard His Father doing, but His answers also established His identity. "Man shall not live on bread alone, but on every word that proceeds out of the mouth of God" (verse 4), and, "You shall not put the Lord your God to the test" (verse 7). And again, "You shall worship the Lord your God, and serve Him only" (verse 10).

I believe Jesus emerged from the wilderness more fully confirmed in His identity as the Son, in the nature of His Father, and in a determination that He would rise to no ambition that would endanger the relationship. Jesus' temptation in the wilderness sharpened in Him a singular hunger for His Father's company that reduced all earthly rewards to insignificance.

After forty wilderness years in which God weeded out unbelief and disobedience, the people of Israel were confirmed in their identity as God's people and in their understanding of Him. With that faith and that secure identity established, they conquered and held their promised land.

I lost a great many years to a faulty sense of identity, not really understanding or believing my chosenness. An old root of rejection blinded me to the revelation that God favored me. I therefore built a fortress of ambition and achievement around that empty place in my heart and even became an abusive leader in an attempt to maintain enough success in my life and ministry to avoid facing my sense of rejection and a consuming fear of it. The wilderness burned rejection out of me, revealed my God to me and set my hunger in order.

A Place of Rest

Jesus said to the disciples, "Come away by yourselves to a secluded place and rest a while" (Mark 6:31). This may sound backward to our acculturated ears, but we must learn to rest in pain and loneliness and to plumb the depths of hunger and thirst. Yield to it and let it do its work as the hand of a loving God doing good for us. He desires more than our service; He longs for *us*. In fact, if He must choose between you and your service, He will choose you every time. Given a choice between the ministry and the man, our Lord saves the man. He can create a ministry with a mere word, but a man or woman is a precious, eternal and beloved child.

I carry a bit of that wilderness, my dark night of the soul, within me all the time, almost as a fragrance or an echo of the path I once walked. It reminds me who I am and teaches me wisdom. Although the suffering has passed, the wilderness remains a place of peace in the midst of the pressures of the ministry where I remember both my own weakness and God's strength. The wilderness reminds me that God is my provider and my Father. In that place I cling to a singular hunger for the pure presence of my Lord. I go back there—or am taken there—whenever I need to renew a sense of peace, when cleansing needs to go deeper or when I have gotten off the track in some way.

Life's labor, once bathed in turmoil and striving, becomes a place of rest after the wilderness. The dark night of the soul brings about the end of self-motivated efforts and solidifies the realization that only the sovereignty of God brings true blessing. Not my talent. Not my ability. Not my anointing. The anointing was never mine anyway.

In the wilderness I came to realize that no matter how good I might be professionally, it amounts to nothing if God chooses not to bless. I can be the best preacher, the best teacher, the most skilled administrator and the wisest pastor, but if God Himself withholds the anointing, there can be no fruit. I have seen God anoint fools and scoundrels to great ministry or success in business while He set wise men on the sidelines simply because of His sovereignty, His mercy and His perfect purposes.

In the wilderness, therefore, God blesses by not blessing, so that you learn what you cannot do and come to rest in Him. He sustains us in the wilderness but holds back the promise for a time, just as He sustained Israel in its corporate wilderness but held them back from the Promised Land until their changed character could sustain the magnitude of the blessing.

A Place of Restoration

Therefore, behold, I will allure her, bring her into the wilderness and speak kindly to her. Then I will give her her vineyards from there, and the valley of Achor as a door of hope. And she will sing there as in the days of her youth, as in the day when she came up from the land of Egypt.

Hosea 2:14–15

After the cleansing fire, after the hurt, after the judgment on my sin, when I come to that singular hunger for the pure presence of Jesus, then I am ready for what the Lord intended all along. I have become a safe steward of it, ready to wield it effectively for the Lord's bride and the good of others rather than destroy it through flesh or foolishness.

The wilderness both digs and lays the foundation for all that must come after. The foundation must go deeper for the building to go higher. Therefore, in preparation for a great work, God digs a deep hole. He is more concerned with forming your character than with building a great ministry, more concerned with the fruit adversity produces in you than with delivering you from it.

In the wilderness the Lord began to grant me the character changes I had asked for all my life. In the wilderness He restored me to myself and to Him when I had become lost in fear, striving, ambition and control.

162

A Place of Preparation

A voice is calling, "Clear the way for the LORD in the wilderness; make smooth in the desert a highway for our God. Let every valley be lifted up, and every mountain and hill be made low; and let the rough ground become a plain, and the rugged terrain a broad valley; then the glory of the LORD will be revealed, and all flesh will see it together; for the mouth of the LORD has spoken."

Isaiah 40:3–5

Ancient Near Eastern roads underwent repairs only when the king was about to visit. A runner would be sent ahead to call the people of the region to make the road smooth. In Matthew 3, John the Baptist identified himself as one sent to call God's people to prepare for the coming of King Jesus by removing the bumps from His highway. He prescribed repentance—character adjustment—as the means of such preparation. Similarly, today we must prepare for His visitation by taking the obstructions, lumps and bumps out of the Lord's highway. As we embrace the wilderness it removes impediments to the Lord's coming in our lives by reducing us to a state in which God alone will satisfy and in which we have given up seeking satisfaction anywhere else. In this state, being with Him is more important than success, and neither personal need nor fear pollute our labors. Without a preparatory wilderness there can be no promised land, no destiny.

⚜ Wilderness Dangers

"Lions and tigers and bears! Oh my!" cried Dorothy in *The Wizard of Oz* as she trudged through the wilderness to see the wizard she felt certain could send her home again. Every step of the way, dangers and pitfalls confronted her and her companions. Obstacles sprang up that had to be overcome. Take care to avoid wilderness threats that have the power to derail or prolong your wilderness sojourn. The Wizard of Oz had no real power to deliver, but our God certainly does.

Anger and Bitterness

Does God expect me to embrace this experience with no bitterness? In the end, yes He does. I learned the hard way that if you still have the strength to be angry with God concerning your suffering, then you have some distance yet to go. Seek God for grace to surrender without bitterness.

Over the years, I gradually burned out on judging God for the way He dealt with me. I no longer had the energy for it—and I was wrong anyway, so what was the point? In the wilderness the people of Israel repeatedly worked up their anger toward God until He burned and bred it out of them. No matter how many miracles of deliverance God led them through, every new obstacle became an occasion to grumble and complain against Moses and God. Our perfect Lord intends only good for us and knows how to bring it about. Wounding by His hand can therefore only be an act of love designed to prepare us for the blessing of our destiny by refining the foundation of our character until real faith takes shape in our hearts.

Erosion of Faith

Is it not ironic that the experience designed to eliminate fleshly impediments to faith could actually result in the loss of faith? In the wilderness I knew for certain that the favor of God had been withdrawn from me and that I could do nothing to restore it. This was my wilderness, my dark night of the soul. As the years of darkness wore on, I forgot that every wilderness is only a passage to the promise on the other side. The faith problem surfaced when God had accomplished in me what He had set out to accomplish. The time had come for the wilderness to end and for me to cross the Jordan River into a land flowing with milk and honey, but I found myself unable to transition out of the wilderness into believing God for the blessing. It was time for favor to return, but I remained mired in the wilderness mentality, believing that God had withdrawn His favor from me and that it would never be restored.

Identify this erosion of faith by the absolute statements it produces. "It is always this way . . ." "This always happens . . ." "God will never . . ." In truth, the wilderness is an act of God's love that prepares you for the greater blessing to come, but wilderness thinking and wilderness unbelief can render you incapable of believing for it or of recognizing it when it arrives.

One of the issues God exposed in me through my wilderness testing was a bitter root expectancy that I would always have to fight my battles alone. My expectation of life and God told me that in the face of real obstacles I would always be on my own. I developed this ungodly belief while growing up with my father. Although he was a good and faithful man, as well as a fine father, when I encountered difficulty, I always fought the battle without his help. As long as this issue remained unresolved in my heart, I could not therefore believe that my Father God would ever back me up or fight for me. This led to fear and striving and not a little domination and control of the people who walked with me.

As God allowed things to come unraveled in my life to expose that flaw, I saw the pattern repeating itself and believed that once again I had to fight for my life without real help. With all my strength I fought to hold things together but ended up in burnout and despair. When the time came for favor to return, I had to repent of the judgment and seek healing. It was time to choose faith again, to believe that my Father God would, indeed, fight for me. And He did.

❂ What if I had allowed my expectation to harden and my bitterness to become permanent, as did that first generation of Israelites in the wilderness? How much blessing, how many promised lands, might I have locked out of my life? My God loves me. In love He disciplined me by means of the wilderness to expose character flaws. He did it in part by leaving me to fight more battles on my own than I could handle in my flesh so that I would break and so that unbelief would be refined out of my character. But when His purposes had been accomplished, He restored His favor over me and it became necessary to choose to believe again. In truth, all of it had been an expression of His favor. He loved me enough to risk me in order to save me. I could have chosen settled unbelief. I could have left the ministry in bitterness. I could have allowed the whole experience to lead me to deny God. Therein lay the risk. But had I not passed through that desert, I would never have reaped its benefits.

Apostasy

In the wilderness, apostasy presents a real danger. In your heart you rage, "I've had enough! I'm bailing out. I didn't have these problems before I was a believer! Jesus doesn't work. I'll quit or I'll opt for a lesser level of Christianity." Jesus said that many are called and few are chosen. This attitude is one reason why few are chosen. A number of years ago a cherished associate who served on my staff resigned in bitterness and left the ministry. I later found that he had abandoned Christianity altogether. His early years in the Lord's service had been anointed and fruitful, but when *pathema* came upon him he abandoned both his calling and the Lord. Called but not chosen!

Rebellion

"I'll fix You! See if I pray to You! I'll just go rent a few porno movies and see how You like that! Where's the nearest liquor store? I just won't talk to You for a while, so there!" You may have said or felt these things.

Or perhaps you determined to do a ministry even though God said no. For instance, God allowed my church in Idaho to behave in just the way that would expose my flaws and eventually move me away to Denver.

I tried to escape the pain and have my own way by planting an extension congregation twenty miles away in Spokane, Washington. Bigger city! Bigger church! Every Sunday I led one service in Idaho and then another in Spokane. I expected Spokane to grow and make me feel better, but God refused to bless my rebellion and I was forced to close it several months later. Because He loves me, God would not allow me to circumvent His plan. Do not ask Him to bless your efforts to defy His will.

Disobedience

In the wilderness, disobedience exerts a strong pull. At one point during a time of crisis God told me to pray morning and evening to bracket the day in prayer. I was not talking to Him at the time and could have refused, but I knew the crisis would then have escalated. God told me to publicly make amends to the elders of our church in Idaho for using and abusing them. What if I had disobeyed? After all, they had done as much damage to me as I had done to them, or so I thought. Or what if I had quit the ministry? I really wanted to, but I could not think of a viable alternative. Blessings would have been lost and character changes would have been delayed. Many confused wilderness leaders do opt out. What tragedy! What loss!

Turning to Other Powers

Many leaders find themselves strongly tempted to turn to forms of illegal force or prohibited sources of power in an attempt to escape the wilderness. Those other sources might be fleshly strength and talent, personal charm or force of will to persuade others. They might be compromised with new-age techniques. Some leaders resort to intimidation. I have seen the Holy Spirit send leaders to the wilderness by causing decline in their ministries, but instead of embracing the suffering, they turned to domination, condemnation and control of their people to try to hold it all together. Or they employed lies and deception to push the "empire" forward. Dishonest fund-raising tactics and hype often become part of the repertoire.

In the family, this same dynamic can manifest as anger, unreasonable demands and emotional or physical withdrawal. Business leaders in the same position sometimes resort to various forms of management by intimidation, or dishonesty in relation to customers, suppliers or tax payments. None of it stands approved by God.

Seeking Relief

We can seek relief in counselor after counselor, conference after conference, new plan after new plan, but the only way out of the wilderness is through it. Attempts at escape can end only as exercises in futility. Relief will be temporary at best and will delay the ultimate resolution.

At the depths of the wilderness suicide can become a strong temptation. The enemy of our soul whispers the lie that the pain of this life can be ended by means of that illegal act. The final chapter of my own sojourn in the wilderness and dark night of the soul began when those elements of my character that the Lord wished to break had been broken. I no longer cared for success. It really no longer mattered to me whether or not I ever again stood on anyone's stage. I needed none of these things. These needs and longings had come to rest, and the time had come at last to deal with my inner woundedness, ungodly beliefs and judgments.

Twenty-seven years of hurt in ministry had filled my pain bucket to overflowing and I could no longer contain or control it. I hurt so badly that I reached a point at which I would have done anything—anything at all—to end it. My parents' fame, however, made it exceedingly difficult to find anyone to effectively minister to me in the manner I needed. Everyone who tried missed the mark so badly that I came out of it more wounded than before. My friend Fred Wright, international coordinator for our church affiliation, Partners in Harvest, at last connected me with Chester and Betsy Kylstra of Restoring the Foundations. The Holy Spirit inspired me to trust them and we set a date three weeks hence to travel to their base in Florida for a time of ministry.

As the days of waiting passed, the pain mounted until one night, in desperation, I found myself lying in bed next to my wife waiting for her to fall asleep so that I could take a handful of pills and end my suffering. Thoughts of the consequences for my wife, my children and the people of my church drew me back from the precipice. I could not bring myself to harm them all and destroy their heritage by taking my own life. I held on.

On my first visit with the Kylstras I worked with them for three days and then later returned for a week, all to deal with old pain that had festered all my life as I controlled and suppressed it, while trying to do the right things with my life. I faced ungodly beliefs and dealt with them. Demons were sent packing. Refreshed and free, I returned to my home and ministry and have remained so in the ensuing years.

Suicide cannot be considered as a way out or as a means of relief. Too many effective healing approaches have been developed over the years for any of us to consider self-destruction as a viable option. Restoring the Foundations (Chester and Betsy Kylstra founders), Elijah House (John and Paula Sandford—my parents—founders) and Shiloh Place Ministries (Jack Frost founder) are just three resources built upon the same foundation. Easy to locate online, all three are Holy Spirit filled and ready to help. These ministries have deployed trained counselors all over the country and internationally. The final stage of your transformation and recovery may just be spending a week with one of these wonderful ministries.

Finally

How long does it take? It takes as long as it takes. Can you shorten the journey? No, but you can make it longer. The difference between redemptive suffering and misery is whether you embrace it or fight it. A friend of mine once joked that the more you complain, the longer God lets you live. Only be certain of the outcome: "For the one who has entered His rest has himself also rested from his works, as God did from His" (Hebrews 4:10).

12

AWED BY THE MYSTERY

The Story of Job

Probably the most difficult book of the Bible to work with is Job, partly because of its complexity, and partly because its message can be so difficult to hear. In a very few verses Job went from prosperity and happiness as a wealthy man honored and respected in his community to absolute poverty and destruction. God granted Satan permission to make it happen, all the while declaring Job a righteous man.

Experiences like Job's often force us to question the fairness and justice of God's dealings with us. I no longer believe God ever promised us fairness this side of the return of Christ, at least not as you and I define fairness. He did promise that He would never leave us or forsake us. He assured us that "God causes all things to work together for good to those who love God, to those who are called according to His purpose" (Romans 8:28). These things I have found to be absolutely reliable, no matter what my senses or emotions have told me in the fiery heat of trial.

Justice is never the issue. Justice would have put me on the cross to bear my own sin. God's idea of justice put Jesus there in my place, though He was innocent of any trespass. Unfair. Unbalanced. Justice has little to do with balance and everything to do with outcome, the realization of God's good and perfect purposes in love.

Overwhelming Losses

As the story unfolds, no part of Job's life escaped ruin. Urgency and fear on his sweating face, a messenger came running to Job with news that as the oxen plowed the fields and the donkeys grazed, raiders came, slew all the servants and made off with the animals. In modern terms we could say that an enemy had murdered his employees and stolen all his tools. Suddenly, Job was out of business. And his other enterprise? Raiders killed those servants, too, and then hijacked all his camels. In one devastating day, both his manufacturing and shipping operations had been wiped out and his financial empire laid waste.

I can imagine Job comforting himself, "Ah, but I still have my family," as another runner breathlessly approached. Between gasps, he reported that Job's sons and daughters had been enjoying their cycle of feasts in one of their homes when a sudden violent windstorm came up and collapsed the house. All Job's children lay buried beneath the rubble. His life. His posterity. Those who would take care of him in his old age. His living retirement plan. Not only were those he loved dead, but neither would anyone be around to support him in his old age. I can only imagine how he must have felt as he searched the ruins, weeping, for the mangled bodies of his beloved children.

Being a righteous man, and having trained himself to turn to God in all things, "Job arose and tore his robe and shaved his head [Jewish expressions of mourning], and he fell to the ground and worshiped" (1:20). Many of us would blame and seek to punish God in the face of this kind of devastation. "See if I come to Your church anymore. I'll just quit praying. See how You like that!" But Job was wholly absorbed in serving his Lord. I call it being wholly owned. So he stowed his feelings away and fell down and worshiped. Later on, anger took root as more disasters befell him and pressures escalated, but at this point he held himself together and did the correct and religious thing.

> He said, "Naked I came from my mother's womb, and naked I shall return there. The LORD gave and the LORD has taken away. Blessed be the name of the Lord." Through all this Job did not sin nor did he blame God.
>
> Job 1:21–22

In other words, Job refused to accuse the Lord of being unfair or inappropriate. In all his wealth, he knew he had possessed nothing but what the Lord had given him and that he had enjoyed it while he had it. Although he grieved his losses, he faithfully chose to confess the Lord's righteousness as good theology dictated he should. As a righteous man dealing with his grief in a righteous way, Job stood his ground. Though his tone later changed somewhat, at this early stage of his long ordeal, he took care to speak only good things. How religiously and theologically correct!

A great deal more pain would come to Job. About to be tested by a level of suffering greater than he could absorb, he had yet to be overwhelmed. Incidents of grief and disaster can sometimes come in such rapid succession, one blow on top of another, that they overpower our human capacity to cope. Suffering can become so intense and so relentless that we can no longer adequately process it. This was about to become Job's experience. God had called him. Freely and without price he had enjoyed his calling and anointing, but he stood now on the threshold of a wilderness exile of suffering and abandonment, after which he would be recalled into even greater prosperity and blessing than he had known before. More importantly, his relationship with God would move to a new plane.

Physical Pain

He passed the first test so well that in chapter 2 God bragged on him: "Isn't Job great? I'm so proud of him!" (paraphrased). But Satan pointed out that God had left him healthy and strong, asserting that if He would allow him to afflict Job's body and ruin his health, it would become quickly and readily apparent what Job was really made of. Satan accused the Lord of unduly protecting Job and stated that without that protection, Job would refuse to serve God at all. In response, God removed the hedge of protection.

Before very long Job came down with the most painful and disfiguring form of disease imaginable. Boils appeared all over his body, injecting poison into his system and inflaming his nerves with unbearable pain. With the boils came a maddening itch. The infection so marred his appearance that people became disgusted at the very sight of him. Maggots began to hatch in his ulcerations as his skin began to blacken and peel. Terrible nightmares plagued him in his sleep. As if to cast a final insult upon an already devastated beggar, the Bible even mentions his bad breath (see Job 19:17).

At last he made his pain-wracked way to the dung heap outside the city, the customary place for those in mourning to roll in the ashes and throw dust in the air. In that place, reserved for outcasts and those expressing extreme grief, Job sat, hour after hour, scraping the puss from his boils with bits of broken pottery and brooding over his fate. In that region of scarcity, water held sacred significance. People therefore believed that the container that carried water retained some of that holiness, and that, as a result, the broken pieces of a water pot contained healing properties. In short, Job tried to doctor himself in the only way left to him.

There on the dung heap, his wife came to mock him in her bitterness and loss, tempting him to curse God and die. He refused, and we hear nothing more of her. His deprivations now complete, Job sat alone.

Friends and Comforters Who Miss the Mark

Friends who came to commiserate found it difficult even to recognize his face. Stunned to silence, for seven oppressive days they sat with him in the dust and dung, uttering not a word. In chapter 3, Job finally broke. In mortal agony of body and soul he cursed the very day of his birth and moaned in despair, "I am not at ease, nor am I quiet, and I am not at rest, but turmoil comes" (verse 26).

This kind of suffering frightens other believers. How could God allow all this disaster to happen to someone who loves Him and serves Him so well; and if He could let it happen to Job, could He let it happen to me? Because it threatened their sense of security, Job's friends could not face that possibility. As a result, fear drove them to theologize Job's sufferings to gain a sense of control over the situation and to reassure themselves that it could not happen to them. In the same way that senseless and relentless suffering frightens us today, Job's condition frightened them and so, by way of offering comfort and counsel, they began to expound their misguided theological understandings of why people suffer. Their arguments sound a great deal like some of the legalistic faith teaching we hear today in some parts of the Body of Christ, and they were every bit as destructive then as now.

Because they held a mechanical view of the nature of God and the causes of both blessing and suffering, Job's friends possessed no adequate theological framework for processing extended and overwhelming human tragedy. They believed that if we would behave just so, then God must bless us, or at least preserve us from serious harm. In that light, Job's condition made no sense to them. "You mean we can't control God?" So after seven days they began to preach, and they called it "comfort."

Formula Faith

Eliphaz spoke first (chapter 4). Like a good many religious fools acting in the name of ministry from that time until this, his offering of comfort included two of the most hurtful assumptions that can possibly be visited upon a sufferer. The first comes in verses 7 and 8: "Remember now, who ever perished being innocent? Or where were the upright destroyed? According to what I have seen, those who plow iniquity and those who sow trouble harvest it."

This is "formula faith" and it goes like this: God rewards righteousness and punishes the wicked; therefore all who suffer deserve it. Faith brings healing; therefore all who are not healed have failed in faith. God prospers those who give faithfully and deal honestly; therefore the poor have done some wrong thing to get that way. If you believe rightly, act rightly, confess rightly and try hard enough, you will be well and wealthy.

This was the theology of Job's day—reflecting their view of how to work the principles of God's Law for personal benefit—and it has become a prominent theology in our own time. One of our oldest heresies, it reduces God to a set of mechanical principles and heaps guilt and condemnation on those He loves when their experience of life does not fit the mold. It takes the mystery out of the majesty of God and reduces Him to something our finite minds can effectively contain. It is an ancient, subtle and insidiously cruel system, and I hate it with all my heart.

God Told Me

As if this were not vicious enough, Eliphaz added the second element. I hear it often today.

"Now a word was brought to me stealthily, and my ear received a whisper of it. Amid disquieting thoughts from the visions of the night, when deep sleep falls on men, dread came upon me, and trembling, and made all my bones shake. Then a spirit passed by my face; the hair of my flesh bristled up. It stood still, but I could not discern its appearance; a form was before my eyes; there was silence, then I heard a voice."

4:12–16

In other words, "I had a dream! God Himself told me why you suffer! Brother, I have a word for you!" So that Job would be both impressed and convinced, Eliphaz shaded the content of this word in mystery, as if the fact that it came cloaked in mystical terms meant it must be God. But mystical experiences are not always divine, and what is not divine can often deeply wound. The ultimate content of Eliphaz's "word from God" was, "You're suffering because you're guilty, because righteous people never suffer these kinds of things."

Eliphaz stated flatly that Job stood under God's discipline, which he obviously deserved (see 5:17–27). Job should simply submit to it and praise God, and then everything would be restored. How nauseatingly simplistic! Confronted with this kind of spiritual excrement, Job's pained and angry reaction was both predictable and understandable. "Then You frighten me with dreams and terrify me by visions; so that my soul would choose suffocation, death rather than my pains" (7:14–15).

Just Pray More and Be Better

Bildad came next. "If you would seek God and implore the compassion of the Almighty, if you are pure and upright,

177

surely now He would rouse Himself for you and restore your righteous estate" (8:5–6). In other words, "Your devotional life is really sad, Job. You need to pray more. If you would only pray more, God would make you a righteous man again."

Job's rebuttal, in what had now become a great debate, asserted that evil men grow wealthy and they die in peace. Paraphrased, he responded, "If what Bildad says is true, then how can this be? Should the evil wealthy person not suffer all these things as penalty for their sin as well? Obviously, the universe does not always work the way Bildad believes it does." If suffering must always be the result of unrighteousness, why do bad guys prosper? Job therefore protested His innocence, and, if innocent, how could he be suffering for some great sin?

How many of us believe that God has withheld our blessing because we have not been good enough? How many of us have heard it said that God cannot bless us because of sin in our lives? But, if that holds true, then who qualifies for blessing? Which of us is ever sinless? And it seems to me that if we did actually qualify, then we would be perfect and in no need of a Savior. In fact, we do not qualify, and for that reason we need Jesus!

Bildad could write a book today that would probably sell a million copies. Its title would read something like *Prayers That Really Work: Five Certain Steps to Health and Happiness*. We could read it, absorb its message and put God in a box. We could push all the right buttons and He would respond by doing everything we want so that we would never have to live with the mystery of suffering, the mystery of His nature or the inscrutability of His ways. But did we forget Isaiah 55:8–9?

> "For My thoughts are not your thoughts, nor are your ways My ways," declares the LORD. "For as the heavens are higher than the earth, so are My ways higher than your ways and My thoughts than your thoughts."

The religious spirit makes a formula out of our relationship with God and denies the unfathomable enigma His nature presents to our limited human understanding. But how could the finite possibly hope to fathom the infinite? How could those whose power, perception and wisdom are limited by their creatureliness possibly fathom the purposes of the Almighty whose power, perception and wisdom know no limitation? How could we who understand so little possibly comprehend the purposes and reasonings of Him who not only knows it all, but created all things from nothing and purposed all things from the beginning?

Whenever we lose sight of the mystery and begin to think we have God and life figured out, we have entered into the religious spirit, and wherever the religious spirit goes, cruelty must ever be close at hand. People inevitably get hurt. Job's friends offered cruel comfort. They had lost sight of the mystery of God and had reduced His dealings to a mechanical set of principles they could control and be comfortable with. They had no paradigm for senseless suffering. The mystery of the nature of God and His dealings was too threatening.

Accusations of Guilt

In a later chapter, Zophar began to speak, angry that Job would claim innocence. According to Zophar, Job suffered less than he deserved because he refused to admit his guilt—which, in Zophar's opinion, must have been present because he would not have been suffering if he were innocent. If Job honestly had no awareness of his personal sin, then God certainly did. Job's suffering could therefore be explained as God awakening Job to repentance. Job was crushed.

God cannot be reduced to a formula. When we reduce our view of God's nature to a set of principles we can manipulate, we inevitably judge and destroy those whose experiences do not fit the formula. Generations of hurting believers have suffered at the hands of those who thought they had it figured out.

When a leader becomes too deeply ensconced in his theology, or too imprisoned in his comfortable understanding of how things work—or ought to work—then he misses God and can become an abuser. God's remedy, the corrective measure of last resort, is often a dark night of the soul, like Job's, that ultimately restores God's servant to mercy, compassion and fellowship with Him, as well as a profound and humble appreciation for mystery.

What Job Knew

Job himself clearly understood two things. (1) He knew for certain that God was responsible for his suffering. At no time did he challenge or question that assumption, and neither did God Himself ever correct it. Job never attempted to split theological hairs or play word games over the issue of whether God directly caused his suffering or indirectly instigated it by allowing Satan to do it. To him it was all God. (2) He knew that no logical reason could be set forth to account for what had happened to him—at least nothing a human being could understand or attribute to any great eternal principle. He knew that he did not deserve his suffering.

He therefore confronted his tormentors in 13:4–5: "But you smear with lies; you are all worthless physicians. O that you would be completely silent, and that it would become your wisdom!" Again in 19:2: "How long will you torment me and crush me with words?"

The kind of religion practiced by Job's friends takes the mystery out of the nature of God and reduces to a formula that which God intended to be a living relationship. When that happens, abuse of the wounded inevitably follows. Arrogance works like that.

The Truth of the Matter

Job longed desperately to understand why God had done all this to him and he argued hurtfully with his friends who thought they held the answers and had solved the mystery. They judged Job guilty. "He suffers; therefore he must be guilty." Because sin does inevitably bear fruit in human suffering, sometimes we can legitimately work backward from suffering to some form of sin that caused it, but the book of Job clearly teaches that this does not always apply.

The Trap of the Religious Spirit

Actually, Job was trapped in the same religious spirit that so blinded his friends. This contributed to the intensity of his agony. Deeply and desperately he searched for a flaw in himself that would explain it all. Had he been able to find something, it would have helped him understand, and he would have been able to chart a course of action in repentance to end it all. But he came up empty-handed, confronted with the impenetrable mystery of the purposes of God. An even deeper despair resulted. I know. I have been there. No imperfection I could discern—and there were and are plenty—could have been serious enough to account for the depth of my experience.

At the end, because the formula would not work, and because understanding refused to come, Job became as angry with God as he had been with his friends. I summarize his attitude as, "I have done nothing to deserve this. I have been righteous, yet I suffer horribly! I don't understand. It's not fair!" Sometimes mercy begins at the point of our willingness to sit humbly before the mystery and say to God and to our brothers and sisters, even in anger, "I don't know. I don't get it."

The Mystery of the Sovereignty of God

For a time, God allowed Job to vent his fury over what he perceived as grossly unfair treatment. When at last God spoke,

His words were a stunning rebuke to human understanding and to pride in our capacity to comprehend. "Then the LORD answered Job out of the whirlwind and said, 'Who is this that darkens counsel by words without knowledge?'" (Job 38:1–2). In other words, "You've spoken many words, argued a lot of theology and made yourselves sound really intelligent, but you fools don't know what you're talking about."

Verses 3–5 follow: "Now gird up your loins like a man, and I will ask you, and you instruct Me! Where were you when I laid the foundation of the earth? Tell Me, if you have understanding, who set its measurements? Since you know. Or who stretched the line on it?"

God went on to list the mysteries of the universe, verse after verse. "Have you ever in your life commanded the morning, and caused the dawn to know its place?" (verse 12). I love the French story *The Little Prince*, about a prince who lived on a planet all his own and over which he ruled as king. He claimed such power and authority that he could actually command the sun to rise. When challenged to prove his sovereignty by doing so, he stated that the conditions were not yet right for obedience. Only at a certain hour would the conditions be right for the sun to obey him. Such is both our human helplessness and our arrogance.

"Is it by your understanding that the hawk soars?" (39:26). What incredible effrontery to suppose that we could fathom the designs of God! Who do we think we are? To really know God is to be confronted with the magnitude of what we could not possibly know. Get used to it! If you would walk with Him in true humility, then you must learn to live with unanswered questions—questions that the finite human mind could never hope to grasp the answer to, no matter how hard we might try.

Yet our suffering often drives us, as Job's drove him, to cry out that God has been unfair! We therefore pass judgment on His dealings. We question the wisdom of what He allows to happen all because we presume to understand!

We rightly believe that God is love according to 1 John 4:8. Knowing this, we presume to comprehend what constitutes love and to judge God for dealing with us in ways that do not appear to be loving according to our limited perception of reality.

In Job 40:8 God puts an end to Job's objections: "Will you really annul My judgment? Will you condemn Me that you may be justified?" God has been unfair? God broke the contract? Do we really think we know better than He concerning the course of our lives and that we have gotten a raw deal out of it? Where were we when He called light into being or set the earth on its course? We do not and cannot understand.

God and His love remain a permanent mystery with good purposes for each of us that we could not possibly fathom or anticipate. In fact, if He ever really tried to tell us what they were, or how He was going to bring them to pass, we would remain profoundly confused and would probably end up angrier with Him than before He gave the explanation. My Osage Nation ancestors were right to name Him *Wah-Kon-Dah*, "the Great Mysteries."

Thousands of galaxies cluster around the known universe, each containing uncounted stars at distances from us and from one another that reduce the human mind to helpless and hopeless confusion. With a word God made it—all of it—ruling it by decree, knowing the movement of every atom of every bit of matter in every star system in every galaxy. Mystery! And we would judge His dealings and challenge His wisdom? We need a new revelation of the mystery and the awe of God, together with the grace to rest in it.

Resolution and Surrender

Then Job answered the LORD and said, "I know that You can do all things, and that no purpose of Yours can be thwarted. 'Who is this that hides counsel without knowledge?' Therefore I have declared that which I did not understand, things too wonderful for me, which I did not know. Hear, now, and I will speak; I will ask You, and You instruct me."

42:1–4

Job begins to get the point: "You're not limited by this stupid theology we humans have been discussing."

We must surrender the human pride that justifies anger with God over things we judge to be unfair in the course of our lives. We must surrender to the mystery, even when it includes seasons we believe to be filled with senseless suffering. The dark night has taught me some understanding, at least, of what the apostle Paul meant when he wrote:

> Not that I speak from want, for I have learned to be content in whatever circumstances I am. I know how to get along with humble means, and I also know how to live in prosperity; in any and every circumstance I have learned the secret of being filled and going hungry, both of having abundance and suffering need. I can do all things through Him who strengthens me.

Philippians 4:11–13

As Job's protests crumbled before the revelation of the awesome nature of God, he surrendered and declared, "I have heard of You by the hearing of the ear; but now my eye sees You; therefore I retract, and I repent in dust and ashes" (Job 42:5–6). He repented for His faulty understanding of God and for believing that he had grasped that which could not possibly be apprehended. At the end of exile and pain, Job found his place again in the scheme of things. Human pride had become divine humility and glorious revelation, and so he entered into a restored peace with God, captivated by the mystery. God got out of the box, and is that not where we really want Him to be? Standing eternally and lovingly above our ability to control Him?

St. John of the Cross, teaching on the seven mansions of the soul, spoke of the beatitude that comes after the dark night—a state of peace, joy and rest with God that truly does pass understanding. My own passage through the dark night has brought me episodes of this at a level I had never before experienced. Because my grip on it can often be tenuous, I must sometimes actively choose to remain in that peace and joy. Occasionally I fail, but the peace and joy remain, waiting for me to return. This has revolutionized my dealing with people, my preaching, my leadership and my handling of crises. My wife is delighted. She has found a resting place in me that she had never known before the wilderness changed me. She deserves it. She waited a long time.

Job's "formula faith" comforters found themselves in big trouble with God, while Job himself became three times as prosperous and blessed as before. Having been captivated anew by the mystery and wonder of the Lord, and having been humbled in his own understanding, he became a safe repository for the blessing God had stored up for him in love all along.

How safe are you and I to receive our blessing, our calling, our destiny? How ready to occupy our promised land? Still judging God? Still thinking we really know? Still preaching great sermons out of our ignorance and fear to those who suffer? I do not know. I know only that there is a lot more to God and His goodness than we can ever learn of or even begin to fathom, and I bow in awe before Him!

EPILOGUE

The first goal of our Christian life, on which everything else depends, has always been twofold: to become like Jesus in all our character, and to walk in true intimate relationship with the Father. On the one hand we have been given the mind of Christ (see 1 Corinthians 2:16). On the other hand certain obstacles stand in the way. "Pursue peace with all men, and the sanctification without which no one will see the Lord. See to it that no one comes short of the grace of God; that no root of bitterness springing up causes trouble, and by it many be defiled" (Hebrews 12:14–15). Roots of bitterness and sinful or unhelpful structures of character keep us from our God-ordained destinies and often harm the people we love, despite our deepest desires to bless them.

Early in my career I helped formulate some of the teachings based on Hebrews 12:14–15 that we now call "inner healing." I used to wonder why so many people could experience so much healing, repentance and forgiveness (both given and received) and yet continue in the depths of dysfunction. I concluded that the answer lies not in healing but in the cross and resurrection. Healing, repentance and forgiveness remain essential, but there can be no substitute for dying and rising in Christ. The old man cannot be healed. He can only share in the Lord's crucifixion. Paul wrote, "For he who has died is freed from sin. Now if we have died with Christ, we believe that we shall also live with Him" (Romans 6:7–8). And again, "I have been crucified with Christ; and it is no longer I who live, but Christ lives in me; and the life which I now live in the flesh I live by faith in the Son of God, who loved me and gave Himself up for me" (Galatians 2:20).

If you have seen yourself in the pages of this book, then know that you have undergone—and perhaps remain in—a process similar to Paul's. The outcome of that death will certainly be just as glorious and life-giving as it was for him.

This has been a book of hope for believers who feel stuck in times of inexplicable suffering, groping for answers. Everything I have written here adds up to the death of structures of character that needed to die to make room for an injection of the nature and character of Jesus. I have never been happier than I am today. My life and ministry are filled with love and fruitfulness that I never could have experienced had I not passed through the wilderness. Yours will be as well. Weeping lasts for the night, but joy certainly comes with the morning (see Psalm 30:5). Favor returns in greater measure. The long, dark night ends with the dawn.

ABOUT THE AUTHOR

R. Loren Sandford grew up a preacher's son in the Congregational church in Illinois, Kansas and north Idaho. As a teenager he played rock music professionally over three states and two provinces of Canada before leaving to attend the College of Idaho. In 1973 he completed a BA degree in music education, then moved to California and attended Fuller Theological Seminary in Pasadena, earning a master of divinity degree in 1976.

Since 1976 Loren has served four churches full-time, successfully planting two of them himself, including New Song Fellowship in Denver, Colorado, where he remains the senior pastor. In 1979 and 1980 he co-directed Elijah House (an international ministry in Christian counseling and counselor training) and continues to be in demand internationally primarily for teaching but also for leading worship.

Initially ordained in a mainline denomination, he has since served in the Vineyard and now is affiliated with Partners in Harvest, a new association of churches associated with the Toronto Airport Christian Fellowship and the renewal centered there. He has served on the International Input Council for Partners in Harvest, oversees the western region for that family of churches and is a recognized prophetic voice within the movement.

In 1991 he was the worship leader for the first Promise Keepers mass men's meeting at the CU Event Center in Boulder, Colorado, and has released eleven CDs of original music, most of it for worship. In addition to the music, Loren is the author of *Purifying the Prophetic: Breaking Free from the Spirit of Self-Fulfillment, Understanding Prophetic People: Blessings and Problems with the Prophetic Gift, The Prophetic Church: Wielding the Power to Change the World* and *Renewal for the Wounded Warrior: A Burnout Survival Guide for Believers*.

Married since 1972, he and his wife Beth have three grown children and eight grandchildren as of 2009. Loren is also a member of the Osage Nation, a Native American tribe centered in Oklahoma.

Loren can be contacted by email at loren@newsongfellowship.org. Visit the New Song Fellowship website at www.newsongfellowship.org or call 303-430-8100.

More on the Prophetic from
R. Loren Sandford

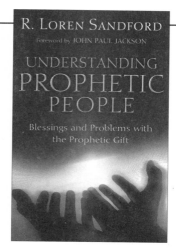

Understanding Prophetic People
by R. Loren Sandford

Insight and Encouragement for Those in the Prophetic Ministry

Scripture lists prophecy as one of five ministry gifts for the Church, but prophetically gifted people have the reputation for being difficult—sometimes impossible—to live and work with. Prophetic pastor Loren Sandford delves into the mysteries of this office and encourages prophets to step out of loneliness and isolation into balance and wholeness. As they grow in their unique calling, the Body of Christ will indeed be blessed.

More on the Prophetic from
R. Loren Sandford

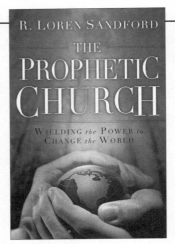

The Prophetic Church
by R. Loren Sandford

Wield the Power to Change the World

It is time to refocus, says renewal leader Loren Sandford, and make the goal intimacy with God. Only as we find His heart will we be empowered to change the culture around us. Providing a powerful vision, Sandford shows examples of what a healthy prophetic community looks like. He helps believers find their place in these "lighthouse churches," places of refuge where people can encounter God's healing and restoration and then go out to transform the culture.